Great Day Trips in The Connecticut Valley of the Dinosaurs

by Brendan Hanrahan

Acknowledgements

The story of the Natural History of Connecticut has always been made richer by people who made it known. Thanks to all who contributed to making this record of the Grand Tradition of Paleontology in the Connecticut Valley.

Suzanne Barabas, Mike Benton, Joe Brenner, Zelda Brenner, Dan Brinkman, Gwyneth Campling, Bill Christensen, Jonathan Craig, Emerson Cooke, Eric Dyer, Meg Enkler, Jim Farlow, Don Farness, Marge Farness, Marilyn Fox, Peter Galton, Adair Garis, Brooks Garis, Chris Garis, Steve Gatesy, Jacques Gauthier, Joyce Gherlone, Eamonn Hanrahan, Georgianna Hanrahan, Nancy Hanrahan, Thomas Hanrahan, Wogan Hanrahan, Phil Huber, Cheryl Izzo, Frank Izzo, Alex Kolezar, Jill Kolezar, Rich Krueger, Donald LaSalle, Alan Levere, Melanie Lewis-Cain, Martin Lockley, Spencer Lucas, John Mazzone, Carol Mahlstedt, Greg McHone, Nancy McHone, Dan McLean, Rachel McLean, Dave McPhedran, Armand Morgan, Barbara Narendra, Paul Olsen, Andrew Perlman, Matt Pretka, Sidney Quarrier, Rick Salwen, Steve Sauter, Will Sillin, David Smith, Lynn Swanson, Mary Ann Turner, Rosemary Volpe, Suzanne Warner, Kate Wellspring.

Road to Discovery Guides is an imprint of Perry Heights Press.

Library of Congress Control Number: 2004092527

ISBN 0-9630181-1-6

10 9 8 7 6 5 4 3 2 1

Contents

How to Use this Book 1

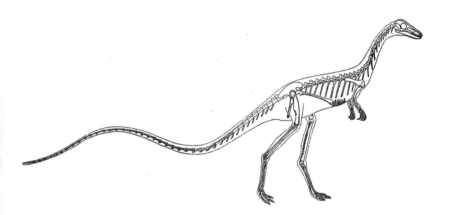

A reconstruction of a Podokesaurus, one of many dinosaurs that existed in the Connecticut valley in the ancient past.
Courtesy, Connecticut Department of Environmental Protection

This book was developed to make it easy for anyone, from families to scientists, to discover the dinosaurs of the Connecticut Valley. Their story is one of strange discoveries and incredible coincidences—tales few people have ever heard.

And yet, the fossils of the dinosaurs, and the stories that go with them, are out there waiting to be rediscovered. Trips to explore their legacies can be made in little more than the time it takes to pull off the highway and eat lunch—and promise to make long-lasting impressions.

This book describes where to go and what to look for at parks and museums up and down the Connecticut Valley in Connecticut and Massachusetts—but it includes much more. There are two parts. The first provides a history of dinosaur science in the Connecticut Valley; the second serves as a guide to top sites.

Trip descriptions are written to stand alone, but are meant to demonstrate subjects explained in the first half of the book. The idea is to have the concepts of dinosaur science explained in introductory chapters come to life during the trips described in the day trip chapters.

The subject of dinosaurs is one that has a way of drawing people in, and the more you know the deeper it goes. Stopping to see dinosaur footprints is always a thrill. You know you're hooked when you begin to wonder whether they were made by predators or prey, how the prints came to be preserved or where it was that the great beasts were going.

To get started, browse the trip descriptions. Thumb through the day trips with your family or friends and find a few places that fit best with the group's interests or plans.

Once a trip is identified, read through the histories presented in the front of the book. The many stories of discovery read more like popular fiction than science or history and are the more remarkable for being true. Read them together taking turns. Discuss favorite parts afterward and these topics will come to life during visits.

With a plan in mind, get in the car and go. None of the sites is far away and all transport visitors to another world.

The Moody Footprint Quarry, South Hadley, Massachusetts, c. 1864
Courtesy, Steve Sauter

I t isn't exactly the kind of place most people imagine when they think of dinosaurs. The Connecticut Valley just doesn't fit an image of a world where bizarre reptiles once menaced their prey, brandishing monstrous teeth and terrible claws.

The surprising fact is there are few better places in the world to explore the early dinosaur era than the central lowlands of Connecticut and Massachusetts. Here, anyone can experience the unique thrill of walking where dinosaurs walked and follow in the footsteps known as *Grallator* and *Eubrontes* (the fossil traces of meat-eating, theropod dinosaurs).

It may be easier to imagine dinosaurs being dug from more exotic or remote locales, like the Montana Badlands or the Gobi Desert of Mongolia, but when it comes to dinosaurs, things aren't always what they seem. The Connecticut Valley may not conjure up enormous bones eroding from windswept, barren hills and deep ravines—but it is where some of the first dinosaur fossil discoveries were made more than two hundred years ago.

Long before dinosaurs were known to science, their footprints were familiar to Connecticut Valley farmers and quarrymen. Fossil footprints and bones have been found in the valley for nearly as long as the United States has been free. They have revealed more and more fascinating details about the origin and evolution of the great beasts ever since. Today, you can learn as much about paleontology (the study of ancient life from fossils) from a drive down the Connecticut Valley as a college student might learn over a semester of lectures—perhaps even more.

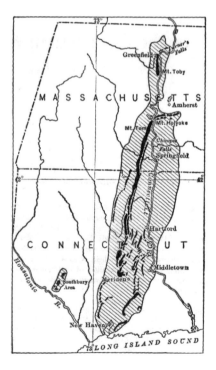

There are many remarkable dinosaur sites to be explored within easy reach. From its northern end, at Northfield, Massachusetts, to where it meets

The Connecticut Valley in Connecticut and Massachusetts (ruled areas). The valley was formed in the Triassic Period by continental rifting associated with the breakup of the ancient super-continent known as Pangaea.
Courtesy, Connecticut Department of Environmental Protection

the Long Island Sound, at New Haven, Connecticut, the valley
is little more than a hundred miles long and twenty miles wide.
Buried within it are abundant fossils of various ancient life forms—
from plants and insects to fish and reptiles. Out West, you could
drive for days and see just a fraction of what can be discovered in an
afternoon in the Connecticut Valley.

The valley is also one of only a few places that an amateur
dinosaur hunter can explore the same sites where world-renowned
paleontologists made famous discoveries. You can see and touch
and explore the same fossils they did. Who knows—you might
even find something the experts failed to notice and help solve one
of the many remaining mysteries about the age of dinosaurs.

A unique place in the world

It's easy to turn a drive through the valley into a trip back
hundreds of millions of years into the past when all the world's
continents were welded into one, great super-continent known as
Pangaea. Here, clues to a world long gone can still be found in the
valley's rocks—if you know where to look.

Learn how the Connecticut Valley, like others from Nova
Scotia, Canada, to the Carolinas, was pulled open when Pangaea
later broke apart. See how this "rift" valley filled with sediment,
lava—and dinosaurs. Discover dinosaurs as they were when they
first grew to dominate life on land—and later in the skies.

Few places can rival the valley for the way it recorded events
from the deep past. Impressions of raindrops that fell 200 million
years ago can still be seen perfectly preserved in stone. They are
just a few of the tens of thousands of trace fossils (footprints, tracks
and marks made by animals and insects) and geological features
common in the valley.

Today, more dinosaur footprints are known from the
Connecticut Valley than any other place in the world. Collections
of fossil footprints at institutions like Amherst College in
Massachusetts and the Yale Peabody Museum in New Haven,

Connecticut, set the standards by which fossil footprint discoveries around the world are measured. No matter where found, from Texas to Poland to South Africa, scientists still compare new finds with footprints first found in the Connecticut Valley.

Perhaps most remarkable is the way the valley's natural "layer cake" of sediments—layers of sandstone, mudstone and siltstone exposed along roads and highways—kept track of time. Thanks to an incredible series of natural coincidences, the valley records a vast span of time, over 30 million years, in thin slices. While fossils known from other parts of the world can only be dated to within a few million years of when they formed, the age of fossils from the Connecticut Valley may be fine-tuned to within a few tens or hundreds of thousands of years.

The color and thickness of the valley's layers reveal how the climate cycled from wet to dry following cycles influenced by fluctuations of earth's orbit. These layers even reveal the world as

An exposure of Connecticut Valley sedimentary strata
Photo: Greg McHone

it was just after a global environmental disaster wiped out much of life on earth—and give us a glimpse of the survivors, including dinosaurs, when life started over.

Past & present

Discoveries made in the Connecticut Valley have shaken things up for centuries. Reports of footprints and bones found in the early 1800s made news around the world. Over the centuries that followed, a small group of local scientists found evidence not only of the existence of dinosaurs, but for such revolutionary, new theories as evolution—theories that changed the way humans imagined the world.

Today, a new generation of paleontologists is at work in the valley. They hope to find answers to questions beyond the nature of local fossils. They want to learn how dinosaurs grew from a few, small animals into a great menagerie of strange and giant beasts. They know nature's next great experiment—the mammals—came along for the ride and can't help but wonder what the dinosaurs' past might reveal about our future.

How does the earth work over very long periods of time? What can we learn from the world as it was early in the age of dinosaurs that might benefit us in our own world today? There are few places in the world to look for answers to what was happening on earth 200 million years ago—and the Connecticut Valley is among the best. As sensational as the first discoveries were two hundred years ago, research being conducted in the valley today promises even more.

The current generation

This book presents the long and remarkable history of geological science in the Connecticut Valley and interviews with the scientists and educators carrying on that tradition today. They are a unique bunch with more than dinosaurs in common. All are fascinated by the valley's secrets and live to see them revealed.

Paul Olsen
Photo: Brendan Hanrahan

Paul Olsen is A. D. Storke Memorial Professor at Columbia University's Lamont-Doherty Earth Observatory in New York. The word fossil once meant anything dug from the ground—and nothing on the ground in the Connecticut Valley, or thousands of meters below it, escapes his scrutiny. Famous for finding fossils where no one else can, Paul's secret is knowing where to look. Perhaps a dozen people in the world know as much about the valley as he does, and most were his students.

The others are specialists in everything from the study of the earth to the study of the planets. They team up with Paul to tackle the valley's greatest mysteries. What they have found so far has led to a new theory for how dinosaurs grew from a few small reptiles to the dominant form of life on earth during the Mesozoic Era.

Spencer Lucas is Curator of Paleontology at the New Mexico Museum of Natural History and Science. Spencer has combed through fossils from North America, to Greenland, Europe, Africa and South America in an effort to understand the "middle ages" of life on earth, especially the Triassic Period. He's laid evidence out chronologically in order to discover how four-legged animals grew and changed around the time dinosaurs first appeared. He has his own ideas about why some prospered and others went extinct.

Steve Sauter, Education Director at the Pratt Museum at Amherst College, Massachusetts, gives tours of the oldest and most important collection of dinosaur footprints in the world, the Hitchcock Collection. His stories make these remarkable fossils even more fascinating and exciting. When he's not giving school groups a tour, Steve is on the hunt for more of his "modern traces." He photographs the marks that everything from worms to birds, tadpoles and people leave in the earth every day, then uses them to teach how dinosaurs made footprints like the ones in the Hitchcock Collection.

Rich Krueger is retired supervisor of Dinosaur State Park in Rocky Hill, Connecticut, where he brought the world of the ancient past back to life. For more than twenty-five years, he's hunted down the descendants of plants that grew in the valley during the age of dinosaurs and found ways of making them grow here again.

Spencer Lucas
Courtesy, Spencer Lucas

He started by reading everything he could about ancient plants and growing small cuttings in his backyard. When they grew tall enough Rich planted them. One plant at a time, he transformed the park back into a place dinosaurs would have loved (to eat).

Peter Galton, Professor at the University of Bridgeport, was a researcher at the Yale Peabody Museum when the trackways at Dinosaur State Park were discovered. Trained in the study of fossil bones, he never

15

expected to study footprints, but the tracks at the park have been a part of his life and work ever since he became involved with them.

Peter still returns to the park to make studies, a remarkable sideline for a paleontologist who is known as an expert on the bones of small, plant-eating dinosaurs (prosauropods) once common in the valley. Over the past few decades he's made significant contributions to the knowledge of the plant-eating dinosaurs of Connecticut.

Sid Quarrier was a geologist with the Connecticut State Survey. He worked with Peter to map the footprints at Dinosaur State Park. Among Sid's innovations was his technique for photographing dinosaur tracks by lashing a ladder to the Land Rover that he and his young family had driven back from Alaska a few months before. From atop the ladder he made the first detailed photos of the site.

Jim Farlow is Professor of Geology at Indiana University-Purdue University at Fort Wayne, Indiana. He became interested in footprints during a trip to Texas one year after a flood exposed a large trackway at a friend's ranch. When he returns to the valley, it's usually to measure footprints at Dinosaur State Park or from the Hitchcock Collection or to work with Peter Galton.

Stephen Gatesy is Associate Professor of Ecology and Evolutionary Studies at Brown University, Rhode Island. He studies the way animals move. A few years ago, he found something in dinosaur footprints no one had ever noticed before. He saw a record of the movement dinosaurs made as they walked, a brief interval of time and motion fossilized in mudstone. These days, he uses features he found in the footprints—along with a few, high-powered computers—to make dinosaurs walk again.

Martin Lockley, Professor of Geology and Paleontology at the University of Colorado, Denver, is a specialist in dinosaur tracks. His own stomping grounds are scattered around the American West. He enjoys the theoretical side of paleontology most, the part

Steve Gatesy
Courtesy, Steve Gatesy

that involves thinking up new explanations for why footprints look the way they do. Martin gets his ideas by looking at tracks and imagining what they might tell him about the way dinosaurs lived and behaved. He asks questions that bones aren't much use for answering. Tracks can—and paleontologists are only beginning to understand how.

Greg McHone is Visiting Assistant Professor of Environmental Science at Trinity College in Hartford, Connecticut. Greg climbs the traprock rock ridges of the Connecticut Valley to sample vast floods of lava he believes once spread through a huge portion of central Pangaea as the super-continent broke up.

The true extent of these volcanic events and what effects they may have had on life in the valley and on earth are not well known. But they have occurred several times in the past and around the times of great periods of extinction. Coincidence or cause? Greg isn't sure, but he believes the great lava floods of the past were too awesome to be overlooked.

Will Sillin says he's a landscape painter, and he is, but he's more than that. Will is perhaps the Connecticut Valley's most accomplished paleoillustrator. He painted the murals at Dinosaur State Park, which was when dinosaurs first got into his blood.

Being a paleoillustrator requires more than just an artist's creativity or a painter's touch. Since most of what remains of dinosaurs is bones and footprints, a paleoillustrator must have a head for paleontology and anatomy as well. He had world-class tutors in Paul and Paul's colleague, Bruce Cornet. Together, they taught him what he needed to know about the valley in the ancient past. Will now uses all of his skills and talents to recreate that prehistoric world. He made the illustrations of the dinosaurs in this book.

Paleontology in the Valley 3

The bust of Edward Hitchcock in front of a Middletown, Connecticut, paving stone with dinosaur footprints raised in relief on the underside.
Courtesy, Pratt Museum of Natural History at Amherst College.

A discovery by a teenager of a slab of brownstone marks a beginning for dinosaur science in the Connecticut Valley. Pliny Moody plowed up the stone at his family's farm in South Hadley, Massachusetts, around 1802. On the slab was a series of odd footprints, like a turkey's, only bigger. The question was, what sort of bird made them? From the look of the tracks, it was unlike any bird seen in the valley before, much less in South Hadley.

No one from Pliny's day could have known what made the tracks. It would be another forty years before three extinct reptiles discovered in England became the first animals ever described as dinosaurs. It wasn't until 1842 that an English paleontologist, Richard Owen, first revealed the existence of the "fearfully great lizards" then being found in England. It would take even longer to connect the small, birdlike animal that left its footprints at the Moody farm with the great behemoths people imagined from the enormous bones in England.

Today, there is little doubt that the footprints Pliny found were those of an early, plant-eating dinosaur—or that they were made long ago, early even for the age of dinosaurs. These were things that could only be known after a long series of discoveries, including Pliny's. Put together over time, these discoveries would change the way people imagined the world.

The world before dinosaurs

Legend has it that after digging up his piece of brownstone, Pliny took it home and put it to use as a doorstep. At least, that's one version of the story about one of the earliest verifiable dinosaur fossil discoveries in history. Much of the rest of the tale has since been given over to folklore.

According to Steve Sauter, the story survives today in various versions. Pliny may have indeed found the stone while plowing his father's field, or he may have pulled it from a streambed elsewhere on the farm. Its slightly worn appearance may be the result of having being trod upon, or it may have been eroded by fast-running stream water. There is even some doubt as to the year Pliny found the stone. Some accounts give the date as 1800, most as 1802 and a few have it as 1803.

It's not surprising that it's difficult to separate the truth of the story from the folklore. The world was a different place two hundred years ago. People held different beliefs. They didn't understand the world as it is known today nor did they have

The brownstone discovered by Pliny Moody around 1802 and dubbed "the Tracks of Noah's Raven." His discovery is today in the Hitchcock Ichnological Collection at Amherst College.
Courtesy, Steve Sauter

the benefit of all that science has revealed over the last two centuries.

Noah's Raven

News of Pliny's discovery spread quickly. A local doctor dubbed the strange footprints "the Tracks of *Noah's Raven*," and the name stuck. It's hard to know what to make of that name today, but according to Steve, people in Pliny's day would have recognized it immediately. They didn't read as many books then as we do today, but one nearly everyone read then was the Bible. Most would have recognized the stone's name from the biblical story of the Great Flood and Noah's Ark.

According to that story, the God of the Bible grew angry with wicked people and loosed a flood of rain to drown the world. Before unleashing his wrath, God commanded Noah to build a boat, the ark, and to bring on board with him two of every kind of animal. Once the floodwaters subsided, Noah, his family and the animals were to disembark and get busy repopulating the earth.

When at last the rains did stop, Noah released a bird to search for land. First he sent a raven, but it never returned and was never seen or heard from again. According to local legend, Noah's raven landed in South Hadley where it left its footprints in the rain-soaked, muddy earth. The tracks Pliny found, or so the story goes, were the tracks of Noah's lost raven.

In spite of the biblical story and local legend, Paul thinks it likely that the name was a sort of local joke. It wasn't anything people took seriously or used to poke fun at Pliny, but it was a way to make light of a peculiar and impenetrable mystery. The name acknowledged that the tracks seemed to have been made a long time before—even if no one knew exactly when.

The age of the earth and the origins of life

Whatever the truth about the story may be, there is little doubt that the name given to Pliny's stone reflected the way many people in the late 1700s and early 1800s saw the world. People's views in those days were often influenced by what they knew from the Bible.

The story of Genesis, for example, tells how God created the world and all living things in six days. This story helped establish long held beliefs about the age of the earth and the origins of life.

As a result, for centuries the earth was thought to be a young planet, barely six thousand years old, and largely unchanged from the time of its creation. An Irish bishop, James Ussher, went so far as to calculate that the first day of creation was Sunday, October 23, 4004 B.C., or not so very long ago.

As for living things, two beliefs were commonly held based on the story of Genesis. One was the notion of fixed species, the idea that since the time of the Creation none of God's living things had been lost or died out and no new ones had been created or evolved. The other was the notion of separate creation, the belief that God created human beings and animals separately and for different reasons. Man was made in God's image to rule the earth. Plants and animals were put on earth for humans to use.

Natural theology

Many early scientists also were influenced by biblical accounts of the creation of the world. They devoted themselves to natural theology, the belief that God could be known and his greatness revealed by the study of his creations: the earth, nature and living things. Natural theology did a great deal to advance the knowledge of the world. It also got some things wrong.

Perhaps natural theology's most lasting contribution was increasing interest in new fields of natural science (then called natural philosophy) among all sorts of people—from painters to poets and from amateur enthusiasts to brilliant scholars. This new interest in turn led to important advances in fields from biology (the study of life), to geology (the study of the earth) and paleontology (the study of the past from fossils). New approaches to classifying and naming plants and animals increased the knowledge about living things, while observations about rocks led to a new understanding of the earth and its geologic features.

When people began looking closely at things around them, however, their observations raised more questions than answers. These questions prompted many Europeans, particularly the French, the English and the Germans, to search for evidence of ancient worlds to discover what it might reveal. Could it be that things appearing impossibly ancient, like mountains and fossils, were formed in just a few thousand years? Or was the earth much older? Were fossils the remains of once living things? If so, was it possible that some of God's creations had died out or vanished? Had the world changed from the time it was created?

Toward a new vision of the ancient past

By the early 1800s, Europeans were making remarkable progress in the search for answers. They led the development of the new fields of geology and paleontology and proposed new theories about the history of the earth. Sixty to seventy years later, long held beliefs about the creation of the world and the origins of life were greatly changed.

Looking at how geological forces shaped and reshaped layers

of rock, the Scottish geologist James Hutton came to believe that the earth was very ancient—far older than previously imagined. His *Theory of the Earth*, published in 1795, argued that "present is the key to the past"—that forces shaping the earth today are the same as those that worked in the past—and that they have been immensely slow. His work influenced generations of geologists and established many fundamental concepts of modern geology.

James Hutton
© *The Natural History Museum, London*

Evidence that extinction had occurred over the now ancient earth's history followed soon after. The French anatomist Georges Cuvier applied his knowledge about the way bones and tissues of living animals went together to describe animals known from fossil remains. He provided proof of extinction by revealing how fossil mastodons were unlike any living relative, such as elephants. In 1796, Cuvier proposed a theory for mass extinctions, suggesting that periodic environmental "revolutions" had wiped out large numbers of living creatures many times in the past.

Cuvier also developed many principles and techniques that remain fundamental to vertebrate paleontology (the study of fossils of animals with backbones). He led the development of the field of comparative anatomy (the study and classification of extinct or unknown animals by comparing them with known animals) and used these comparisons as a means of judging how closely animals were related. An important corollary to the comparative method is the principle of the correlation of parts. Cuvier was skilled in its use. This principle relies on the observation that in nature many different animals share parts of similar design. The more two animals resemble one another, the more closely it may be assumed they are related since their body parts are of a similar design. The concept is essential to classifying fossils and reconstructing animals from partial or incomplete fossil remains.

Another important piece of the puzzle fell into place in 1815 when an English engineer and canal builder, William Smith, drew a connection between Hutton's ancient rocks and Cuvier's extinct animals. He realized that specific kinds of fossils occurred during particular intervals of time in the past. Smith used this observation, known today as the principle of faunal succession, to correlate and to determine the ages of different layers of bedrock under England and parts of Scotland and Wales based on the fossils buried within—an approach known today as biostratigraphy.

The work of Hutton, Cuvier, Smith and others laid the foundations for modern concepts of geology and paleontology. Techniques for describing and dating fossils based on their ideas are still used today. Their ideas also helped to establish timelines for the ancient past and analytic approaches that could be used to identify fossils, including those of dinosaurs, found anywhere in the world.

Their work helped clear the way for a radical new theory about life that came to be known as evolution by natural selection. As more of the past came to be understood, fossil evidence was used to prove that the earth had indeed undergone great changes in the past and that, over time, living things were capable of changing as well.

The early Connecticut Valley discoveries

Against this backdrop, the first dinosaur fossil discoveries in the Connecticut Valley were made. Beginning with Pliny Moody and the discovery of *Noah's Raven* around 1802, and culminating with Edward Hitchcock's *Report on the Sandstone of the Connecticut Valley* in 1858, events in the valley coincided with and helped support important advances being made in Europe.

Less than a year after Hitchcock's report, Charles Darwin ushered in a new era with the publication of his book, *The Origin of Species*, in 1859. Darwin would find support for his ideas in the work of a later generation of Connecticut-based paleontologists. "Your work . . . on the many fossil animals of North America has afforded the best support to the theory of evolution . . ." Darwin wrote to Othniel Charles Marsh, curator of the Peabody Museum in 1880. Others continue to push the frontiers of earth science with research being conducted in the valley today.

Science in the New World

That footprints were even known from the valley was remarkable given that until Pliny Moody made his discovery, little was happening in terms of science in the United States. The United States in 1802 was still a new and very young nation, preoccupied with the business of establishing its democracy. It had a long way to go to catch up with scientific advances being made in the more established European nations.

American medical schools taught sciences like chemistry and anatomy to aspiring physicians, but a quarter century after the American Revolution, no college offered classes in geology. America's first geologists and paleontologists were self-taught and relied on their wits and intuitions.

Events following Pliny's discovery helped change all that. Had he recovered his fossil even a few years earlier it may easily have been overlooked, destroyed or lost. As it was, his discovery proved to have been made at the right time and in the right place. It coincided with a scientific awakening in the United States that began in the Connecticut Valley and was led by a few local scholars. Their efforts mark the beginning of a long tradition of geology and paleontology, one that shifted the center of dinosaur science out of Europe and into the eastern United States in less than a century, where it thrives today.

Incredible coincidences

The story of the Connecticut Valley's dinosaurs is about more than discoveries of fossil footprints and fossil bones. It's actually a story of incredible coincidences. A long and unlikely series of events, beginning nearly a billion and a half years ago, made the valley into a place perfect for preserving living traces and turning bone into stone.

Geologic events that might occur once in a few billion years not only happened here, but continued to happen, one after another and in just the right way, for a thousand million years— from the time the bedrock of New England was first laid down.

This incredible history became known through a series of human events no less incredible than the natural events leading up to them. Pliny Moody couldn't have been further from the scientific revolution of the early 1800s if he'd been plowing fields on the moon—and yet his discovery couldn't have come at a better time or in a more fortuitous place.

Right place, right time

One remarkable coincidence was that at the same time Pliny was working the family farm in the north valley of Massachusetts, plans to open a school of science were being made just to the south, at Yale College, in New Haven, Connecticut. That same year, 1802, Yale hired a young graduate, Benjamin Silliman, to begin teaching chemistry and natural history. Within a few years, Silliman made Yale the first American college to offer geology and to establish a fossil collection—one that would come to include some of the first verifiable dinosaur bones found in North America.

In the fifty years that followed, Silliman went on to pioneer the sciences of geology, mineralogy and paleontology in the United States. He became a leading advocate of science in early nineteenth century America and inspired many people, from ordinary citizens to scholars, to become interested in these subjects as well.

By 1804, Silliman had begun training the first generation of American geologists—and future paleontologists—just a short journey down the valley from the Moody farm. His students later came to have a profound influence on natural science in New England and around the world. They began their training at the same time that the "Heroic Age" of modern geology, the period from 1790 to 1830, gathered steam in England. During this time, the English made many contributions to the knowledge of the earth and fossils. Discoveries of fossil bones along the English coast and countryside promised more.

The first Connecticut Valley discoveries were also made during this time. The accounts Silliman published helped open a dialogue between the English and their young, American colleagues. In the years that followed, the Americans made many trips to the British Isles and the English were greatly influenced by expeditions they made to the Connecticut Valley.

Among those who came to New Haven to train with Silliman was Edward Hitchcock. Hitchcock, a self-taught geologist, became intrigued with the fossil footprints that were common in the valley—including many from the Moody farm—and made the study of tracks and trace fossils his life's work. His first report on the tracks, published by Silliman in 1836 created a sensation around the world.

By the time he died in 1864, Hitchcock had collected and catalogued over 1,200 stone slabs containing some 20,000 footprints and other trace fossils. He published detailed descriptions of many different trackmakers, single-handedly inventing ichnology (the study of fossil footprints).

The tradition of dinosaur science in the Connecticut Valley that was started by Silliman and Edward Hitchcock has continued ever since, led by many renowned American paleontologists. Othniel Charles (O. C.) Marsh, a Yale graduate who met Silliman during early planning for what would become the Yale Peabody

Museum, went on to become one of the most famous—and infamous—of paleontologists. The immense dinosaur skeletons he had collected and shipped to New Haven shaped popular conceptions about dinosaurs. Often overlooked is that Marsh also collected and described several dinosaurs and other reptiles from the Connecticut Valley. These contributions remain essential to the knowledge we have of early forms of dinosaurs today.

Marsh, who died in 1899, was succeeded in 1906 by Richard Swann Lull who continued the study of local fossils well into the 1950s. He reevaluated the Connecticut Valley footprints in light of new discoveries and knowledge.

John Ostrom revitalized dinosaur science during his term as curator of the Peabody starting in the 1960s. Where dinosaurs had been seen as dull-minded, lumbering behemoths, Ostrom found evidence that some, like the raptor dinosaur *Deinonychus*, were likely much smarter, faster and more agile than had been presumed. He also resurrected old debates over similarities between reptiles and birds that began with Hitchcock and Owen and were later fueled by Marsh. Ostrom's comparisons of *Archaeopteryx*, the earliest known bird, and *Deinonychus*, was one of the most influential arguments for the hypothesis that birds are the descendants of meat-eating, theropod dinosaurs.

Ostrom's influence is still felt in the Connecticut Valley. Many who carry on the tradition of dinosaur science here today, including Jacques Gauthier (Ostrom's successor as curator of the Peabody), Peter Galton, Jim Farlow, Spencer Lucas, Paul Olsen and others, were greatly influenced by Ostrom, his ideas and his work.

The Grand Tradition 4

Reconstruction of the Connecticut Valley dinosaur Anchisaurus
Courtesy, Connecticut Department of Environmental Protection

Discoveries made in the Connecticut Valley have always been big events—and there have been many made here over a long period of time. Together they trace a grand tradition of dinosaur science that began in the valley and has continued for centuries.

The tradition got its start during Thomas Jefferson's first term as President of the United States and before Lewis and Clark left on their expedition up the Missouri River. Early distinguished paleontologists searched the ancient past here, and their work is carried on today by scientists with roots in the Connecticut Valley.

Yale University Art Gallery. Gift of Bartlett Arkell, B.A. 1886, M.A. 1898, to Silliman College

Benjamin Silliman and "the Bones from the Well"
The earliest verifiable discovery of dinosaur bones in North America
Partial skeleton
Prosauropod dinosaur
Yale Peabody Museum catalog number YPM 2125

"Mr. Solomon Ellsworth, Jun. Of East-Windsor, (Conn.) has politely favoured me with some specimens of fossil bones, included in red sand stone. Mr. Ellsworth informs me that they were discovered by blasting in a rock for a well."

—Professor Nathan Smith, 1820

So read the note Silliman published in the *American Journal of Science* that November. At first, he thought the discovery of the bones "cannot be considered as very interesting." He didn't know it then, but nearly two centuries later the bones would remain the earliest verifiable discovery of dinosaur bones in North America.

"The bones were evidently those of a perfect and considerably large animal," Silliman noted. They had been found two years earlier, in 1818, after several fragments were exposed during blasting at a location later recorded as "near Ketch's Mills." Their discovery remains obscure to this day—even among paleontologists.

Few dinosaur books even mention "the Bones from the Well" or their significance. Even less is known about the contribution Benjamin Silliman made to paleontology when he acquired the specimen for Yale College. Silliman had "the Bones from the Well" examined by Yale Medical School professors, and published some of the earliest known descriptions of what would eventually be recognized as a dinosaur in the *American Journal of Science.*

Another skeleton discovered in England at about the same time grabbed headlines instead. The bones of *Megalosaurus* are believed to have also been collected that year or earlier by the English geologist William Buckland at a site near Oxford University, England. It took several years for Buckland to report his discovery, but the report he finally published in 1824 is now considered one of the first scientific descriptions ever made of a dinosaur.

As long as it took Buckland to describe *Megalosaurus*, Americans spent decades poring over "the Bones from the Well" before O. C. Marsh declared them to be dinosaurian in 1896. "The remains of dinosaurs first discovered in this country were found in the Triassic sandstone of the Connecticut Valley, so famous for its fossil footprints . . ." Marsh noted in *The Dinosaurs of North America.* ". . . It is a remarkable fact that the first discovery in this sandstone was that of the skeleton of a true dinosaur, found in East Windsor, Connecticut, in 1818, many years before the first footprints were recorded."

The well's location fell into obscurity until it was rediscovered in 1988. Unfortunately, the site lies on private property where it is inaccessible to the public.

Silliman & paleontology

The descriptions Silliman published of "the Bones from the Well" in the *American Journal of Science* stand among the first of a dinosaur in North America. He continued to publish new studies of the bones and later finds throughout his career, including the first scientific study of fossil footprints in 1836.

"It is to be hoped that the pieces of the bones, when they are cleared of the rock that incloses (sic) them, will enable us to ascertain the fact whether they are human bones, or the bones of brute animals," Nathan Smith wrote in the note Silliman published.

In fact, the bones were recognized as animal by a local surgeon who was there as the bones were being brought up. "Doctor Porter was present a considerable part of the time while the well was digging," John Hall, of Ellington, Connecticut, wrote to Silliman in reply to the published report, "and had the best opportunity for forming a judgment of the nature of these bones."

The bones began to crumble almost as soon as they met the air and Porter had the best look at them that anyone ever will. Today, the fossils are seen as little more than chalky streaks that contrast sharply with the dark, red sandstone that still surrounds them.

"[Dr. Porter] says that the bones did not belong to a human body, but to some animal," Hall continued, "and that the animal must have been about five feet in length. The tail bone was easily discovered . . . by its being projected, in a curvilinear direction beyond the general mass."

At the time, few large animals like the one whose bones were found in the well were known. Mary Anning and her brother, two members

"The Bones from the Well"
(YPM 2125).
Copyright©2004 Peabody Museum of Natural
History, Yale University, New Haven, CT

of England's famous fossil-hunting family, had discovered the skeleton of one of the earliest known marine reptiles, *Ichthyosaurus*, only a few years before. Discoveries of other extinct reptiles soon followed, including another large dinosaur (later named *Iguanodon*), by Gideon Mantell in 1822. It would be decades before the nature of these reptiles and their relationships to others, such as the one found in East Windsor, came to be understood.

Edward Hitchcock, who trained under Silliman, was among the first to connect "the Bones from the Well" and others found nearby with reptiles. "I suspect these bones belonged to a saurian animal,'" he wrote in 1835, referring to a group of reptiles by their scientific classification. He wondered later if they might not somehow be related to Buckland's *Megalosaurus*. "Can it be the specimens under consideration are of the same nature?" he wrote in 1841. "The hollow character of the bones certainly favors this idea."

Dr. Jeffries Wyman, whom Hitchcock esteemed "a far better judge than myself," affirmed the reptilian nature of the bones in 1855. Wyman had a surprisingly modern take on "the Bones from the Well," having compared them with those of birds, crocodiles and the dinosaurs then known from England, and was the first to conclude they were those of some kind of fossil reptile. "It is a caudal vertebra of a Saurian reptile … and more nearly to those of the Crocodiles than any others," Wyman wrote of a backbone.

"The Bones from the Well" were identified as those of a prosauropod dinosaur after similar types of dinosaurs were found at the Charles O. Wolcott Quarry at Manchester, Connecticut, in the 1880s and 1890s. It's impossible to know what species it was, but Peter Galton says it was related to other dinosaurs known from the valley, including two genera Marsh described later as *Anchisaurus* and *Ammosaurus*. More recently, a researcher from the Bernard Price Institute in South Africa has argued it is more closely related to the prosauropod dinosaur *Plateosaurus* known from Europe.

35

Silliman the pioneer

"Hang up your coats, gentlemen," Benjamin Silliman's son remembered his father telling his students. "My father used to say that if his pupils hung up their coats in his classroom they were sure to take a little chemistry out with them when they left."

Silliman devoted his life to seeing that people from all walks of life took a bit of science away with them. From the Yale students who packed his classes to crowds that filled public halls to hear him lecture, he shared his love of chemistry and the study of the natural world with everyone he could.

Before Silliman began his career as professor of "Chymistry" and natural history, Yale was a college dedicated to the study of the classics and theology. By the time he retired fifty-one years later, Yale came to be highly regarded for its science department and the many great scientists who were educated there.

"Now that I have traveled from Niagara to Georgia," the renowned English geologist Charles Lyell wrote to Silliman in 1842, "and have met a great number of your countrymen . . . I may congratulate you, for I never heard as many . . . refer as often to any one individual teacher as having given direction to their taste."

Son of the revolution

Benjamin Silliman was born on August 8, 1779, in what is now Trumbull, Connecticut. The American Revolution was then mired in its fourth year. Silliman's father, a brigadier general in charge of defending the southwestern Connecticut coast was taken prisoner by the British two months before he was born.

"On a Sabbath morning in May, 1779 the Silliman house was violently assaulted . . . and General Silliman was carried away a prisoner," wrote Robert Dudley French. "Some two months later, Benjamin was born—into a land in violent tumult and a household which had tasted the bitterness of the separations of war." Their way cleared, British troops burned the coastal towns of Fairfield and Norwalk that summer.

Life for the family slowly returned to normal after the war. Silliman's father resumed his law practice. At age 17, Benjamin enrolled at Yale. He graduated in 1796 and worked for a while on the family farm.

In 1798, Silliman was stunned to receive an offer of a professorship in "Chymistry" and Natural History from Yale President Timothy Dwight. Prior to this offer, Silliman had no training in science. At age 23, Silliman was given responsibility for creating the college's first science department.

Benjamin Silliman
Courtesy of the Peabody Museum of Natural History, Yale University, New Haven, CT

He leapt at the opportunity. Silliman traveled the States to attend lectures and study with experts on everything from chemistry to anatomy and surgery. He sailed the Atlantic to consult with Britain's leading scientists. A quarter century after his father sought the British along the Connecticut coast, Benjamin sought them out again, this time to teach him whatever they could of science and natural history.

The relationships he forged then and later nurtured, proved invaluable to science in the valley and in the United States. Within a few years, Silliman was teaching a course on chemistry, mineralogy and geology, and training the country's first geologists and paleontologists.

Accomplishments

Silliman made many contributions to science outside the lab. He published the first scientific study of Connecticut geology, described fossil fish from the valley and even described pieces of a space rock known as the "Weston meteorite."

In writing about the geology of New Haven, he came to recognize the differences between the ancient metamorphic rocks of the highlands to the east and west and the much younger sedimentary stones and volcanic, "traprock" ridges of the valley.

Perhaps the best measure of his accomplishments was his influence on his students. His son Benjamin, Jr. and son-in-law James Dwight Dana also became professors at Yale. In addition to his footprint studies, Edward Hitchcock completed the first geological survey of Massachusetts and became president of Amherst College. James Gates Percival made the first systematic survey of the geology of Connecticut, and his work remains startlingly accurate. Amos Eaton was professor of geology at Williams College and Rensselaer Polytechnic Institute. He conducted a geological survey of New York State. Denison Olmstead supervised a geologic survey of North Carolina.

Silliman also played a founding role in establishing the Peabody Museum. It was he who first went to George Peabody, the wealthy philanthropist, in 1857 and made an impassioned plea for help funding a new science building. He thought his effort had failed, but in 1866, two years after Silliman's death, Peabody made a gift of $150,000 to Yale for the construction of a natural history museum. Earlier, he had appointed Silliman, his nephew (O. C. Marsh) and several others as trustees to "found and maintain a museum of natural history, especially of the departments of zoology, geology and mineralogy."

Silliman was involved with the early planning of the museum until shortly before his death. He died peacefully at his home in New Haven on Thanksgiving Day 1864, on "a day of belated summer warmth."

Edward Hitchcock & the 3,000-year-old turkey tracks
Tracks of "the turkey tribe"

> *"In March, 1835, Mr. Draper, of Greenfield, Massachusetts...*
> *noticed on some slabs of flagging stone ... impressions which he*
> *described [as] '. . . turkey tracks made 3,000 years ago.'*
> *"Mr. Wilson showed them to Dr. Deane, who described them*
> *to me by letter: 'In the slabs of sandstone from Connecticut River...*
> *I have obtained singular appearances . . .One of them is distinctly*
> *marked with the tracks of a turkey (as I believe) in relief. There*
> *were two birds side by side making strides of about two feet.'"*
>
> —Edward Hitchcock

Three thousand-year-old turkeys? That walked with strides
two feet long? If Deane was right they must have been some
turkeys. As preposterous as the message may have seemed to
Edward Hitchcock, it must have been equally irresistible. A bird
that took two-foot steps would have to be big—perhaps as big as a
man—much bigger than any seen in the Connecticut Valley before.

"In reply to [Dr. Deane's] letter," Hitchcock wrote, "I stated how interesting these impressions would be if they turned out to be real...I went to Greenfield a few days after, and a glance at the specimens satisfied me that they were deserving of careful examination. That they had the appearance of tracks no one could doubt, and they bore a strong resemblance to those of some kind of birds. I secured the specimens and determined to enter upon the most careful examination of the subject by every means in my power. That investigation I have now been carrying on for twenty-three years..."

On that day in Greenfield, the field of ichnology (the study of fossils footprints) was conceived. Edward Hitchcock's work set a standard for comparing subsequent work on all other fossil footprints nearly two centuries later.

"I am much gratified that you are seriously at work upon the turkey tracks, or bird tracks, or whatever kind they may be," Silliman wrote to Hitchcock. "My impressions are so strong in favor of the genuineness of the discovery—judging only from the imperfect copy I have in plaster—that I feel exceedingly desirous to have the matter investigated; and I do not know in whose hands it can be better placed."

Nature's healing powers

Edward Hitchcock lived a life of passion and struggle set out for him early on. He was always driven by a great hunger for learning, but the more he sought to satisfy his curiosity for religion, classic literature, ancient languages and science, the worse the pains in his belly grew to be.

Hitchcock was born on May 24, 1793, in Deerfield, Massachusetts, the heart of the north valley. His father was well respected, "but he had to struggle hard with a trade not very lucrative, to feed, clothe, and educate a large family," Hitchcock wrote. "He had commenced his family career during the Revolutionary War, in which he had been twice engaged as a soldier, as was his father, who fell a sacrifice to the diseases of the camp."

Following in his father's path, Hitchcock grew to be a devout Christian, but discovered a passion for science as well. "I had acquired a strong relish for scientific pursuits," he wrote, "and I seized upon every moment I could secure—especially rainy days and evenings—for those studies. I was treated very leniently by my father and brother, who probably did not know what to do with me, but saw plainly that I should not become distinguished as a farmer."

As a young man, he loved to stay up nights and scan the sky, especially for a glimpse of the "great comet of 1811." But by the time he was 18, pains in his stomach were so unrelenting they made stargazing impossible. "I was engaged in making observations… on the comet's distances from the stars," he recalled. "I gave myself to this labor so assiduously that my health failed… When my physician was consulted he said, 'I see what your difficulty is; you have got the comet's tail in your stomach.'"

Hitchcock's condition only worsened. In 1814, a bout of the mumps left him blind and weak and forced young Hitchcock to abandon his dream of enrolling at Harvard and getting a college education. "It almost completely cut me off from all literary pursuits, and for forty years it held its grasp upon me so firmly, that scarcely ever could I use my eyes for an hour without pain…cutting down my ability to study."

He regained his sight in 1816 and was taken in by Deerfield Academy where he continued his studies and trained to enter the Christian ministry. "I laboured intensely," he wrote, "to maintain myself in spite of a defective education, weak eyes, and poor health."

In nature he found strength. Hiking in the mountains around Deerfield proved more therapeutic than any doctor's treatment. "Excursions in the fields and the mountains … have ever since been with me a most important means of resisting the progress of disease," he wrote. Making his way up the trails, Hitchcock developed a fascination for the natural history of the valley which occupied him for the rest of his life.

Hitchcock made frequent field trips to learn all he could about the natural history of the valley. In the hills, Hitchcock collected rocks and plants. Whatever he found interested him. He began attending lectures at Amherst College and became acquainted with many local scientists, including Amos Eaton, one of the young generation of geologists who had studied at Yale with Silliman. He became an expert on the natural history of the valley. Despite his lack of formal scientific education, his observations about the geology of the north valley earned him notice. The young Hitchcock became one of the earliest contributors to the *American Journal of Science* when Silliman published his report on the geology and mineralogy of the north valley in 1818.

Professor of Chemistry and Natural History

As passionate as Hitchcock was about geology and natural history, in his heart science took second place. His true calling, he felt, was the Christian ministry, "having been led by my trials to feel the infinite importance of eternal things… "

He was appointed minister of a parish in Conway, Massachusetts, in 1821, but after a few years his duties left him exhausted and too ill to continue. He reluctantly resigned and accepted a position he hoped would not exact so great a toll. "About the same time the Trustees of Amherst College, knowing my penchant for science, appointed me Professor of Natural History and Chemistry."

In the fall of 1825, Hitchcock left for New Haven to study chemistry with Benjamin Silliman at Yale. He returned to Amherst reinvigorated, only to realize the challenges awaiting him. "When I joined the College in the winter of 1826, there was no laboratory… no natural history cabinet [a scientific collection] and no chapel."

AMHERST COLLEGE.

Undaunted, Hitchcock began to lecture in zoology (the study of animal life), botany (the study of plant life), chemistry (the study of the properties of physical substances), geology and anatomy (the study of the structure of living organisms). What he didn't know, he taught himself. What apparatus, models or specimens the college lacked he found ways to provide.

Fossil footprints and the science of ichnology

By 1835, Edward Hitchcock had been professor at Amherst College for ten years. He was a prolific writer and his reputation had grown considerably. He was appointed Geologist to the State of Massachusetts and became known for his many contributions to the *American Journal of Science* and other journals.

Hitchcock observed differences in the traprock ridges prominent up and down the valley. He proposed that some were formed by lava pressing up from cracks, or faults, in the earth's crust, rather than exploding from a volcano. It took years for his ideas to be accepted, but Hitchcock had anticipated what geologists know today as fissure eruptions. Never one easily deterred, Hitchcock was not reluctant to submit his ideas to the scrutiny of the scientific process or of other scientists, even though the most important work of his career (describing hundreds of previously unknown fossil footprints) would prove highly controversial.

43

Inventing ichnology

Hitchcock took up the study of footprints soon after seeing Deane's stone in Deerfield. "After visiting all the quarries in my power during that summer," he wrote, "I ventured to give a scientific description of seven species in 1836. With a few eminent exceptions [including Benjamin Silliman and William Buckland, the English geologist who discovered *Megalosaurus*] my views were not adopted by scientific men. Yet, I continued to explore and from time to time describe, new species, till within six years, in which I labored almost alone ... they amounted to thirty-two, and a general acquiescence was secured among scientific men in the views that had been advanced."

Hitchcock's first study entitled *Ornithichnology*, a term Hitchcock coined to mean the study of "stony bird-tracks," was big news on both sides of the Atlantic. In it he described seven different kinds of fossil footprints.

Some of the impressions he examined were so well preserved they appeared freshly made. Some took detailed molds of the skin of the animals' feet. Others even showed smudges in places where the animal's foot had moved through the slimy mud. Most allowed Hitchcock to conduct scientific analyses. He counted the number of toes and made measurements of the size and shape of the foot. He noted whether the animal appeared to walk on two feet or four, whether its feet were webbed or clawed, the length and width of its strides and more—over 30 fields of data in all.

Birds, reptiles and trackmakers

Hitchcock's studies led him to conclude that many of the impressions he catalogued were the footprints of large, flightless, long-extinct birds. They had a distinctly birdlike appearance, a sort of trident formed by the impression of three toes and found in sizes from small, to medium, to large. The largest were 18 inches long, heel to toe, and deep enough to hold a gallon of water.

Hitchcock found many specimens containing a series of footprints, or tracks, made by an animal walking through mud. The impressions showed that many of the trackmakers walked on two feet. The strides they took as they walked were much greater than those of living birds, but otherwise looked much like the footprints turkeys left in farmyards every day. Because the footprints were impressed in brownstone, Hitchcock estimated that birds, along with many other animals, lived in the valley during what was known then as the oolitic series—or the age when the red sandstone was put down in the valley, perhaps 50,000 or 100,000 years earlier.

Hitchcock realized many would find his claims absurd, but he believed he had the evidence to support them. After all, he'd been skeptical himself when Dr. Deane first wrote him about the tracks, but was quickly persuaded upon seeing them. He came to understand what it was to gaze at a footprint for the first time, to be taken in by it and overwhelmed by the mysterious testament it offered.

"I threw it aside at first," Hitchcock wrote of his initial encounter with a large footprint, "because I could not believe that an impression three or four times larger than that of the great African ostrich's foot, could be a track. But this animal turns out to have been one of the most common of all that trod upon the muddy shores ... I regarded it as the giant ruler of the valley."

Hitchcock's Eubrontes.
Courtesy, Paul E. Olsen

The footprint he later designated *Eubrontes* is now thought to have been a large meat-eating dinosaur.

Many geologists tossed Hitchcock's report aside. Some contended the shapes in the Connecticut Valley sandstones weren't tracks at all. Others argued it was impossible to know with any certainty what animal might have made them. Fossil bones were proof positive; tracks were little more than Mesozoic mud pies.

Eventually, seeing was believing for Hitchcock's reviewers, just as it had been for him. It was difficult to argue with Hitchcock's conclusions after looking at the dozens of stone slabs he had collected, all filled with footmarks. A committee of the American Association of Geologists and Naturalists was so impressed, they concluded in 1841 that "the evidence entirely favors the views of Professor Hitchcock." Two of England's most renowned scientists, the geologist Charles Lyell and the anatomist Richard Owen, were also intrigued by the footprints that they journeyed to the valley to see.

Birds & dinosaurs

Hitchcock kept in touch with Owen throughout the remainder of his career. It wasn't clear to them then, but each was working different sides of the same problem—the reptile-bird connection that still fascinates paleontologists today. Both were on trails that led to important discoveries and contributed greatly to knowledge about dinosaurs—Hitchcock by following in their footsteps and Owen by piecing together their bones.

Owen was renowned as a brilliant anatomist—and nearly as famous for having a nasty disposition. In the tradition of the French anatomist Georges Cuvier, Owen spent decades studying animal anatomy (the characteristics of bones and tissues and the way they go together). He didn't doubt Hitchcock's footprints were real, but was uncertain as to whether they were the marks of birds or of reptiles with birdlike features.

Owen's great skill was in applying methods of comparative

anatomy in order to sort animals into groups or taxa. He became known for using these techniques to describe and sort extinct animals based on fossil bones and bone fragments.

When Hitchcock's *Ornithichnology* was published in 1836, Owen was on the verge of making many great contributions to paleontology, including several that eventually helped unlock the mysteries of the Connecticut Valley footprints. He is best known as the man who described a group of bizarre, extinct reptiles as dinosaurs or "terrible lizards" six years later, in 1842.

Hitchcock had great respect for Owen. As difficult as others found Owen, Hitchcock had only praise for him. Hitchcock was greatly influenced by a claim Owen made a few years before he described dinosaurs—one based on a small fragment of bone from New Zealand. Owen recognized the similarity between the fragment and a leg bone of an ostrich. It led him to conclude in

1839 that large, flightless birds had lived in New Zealand before they went extinct. More bones found later enabled Owen to describe the bird as *Dinornis*, a kind of moa, in 1843.

To Hitchcock, *Dinornis* looked like a dead-ringer for the bird he took to be "the giant ruler of the valley." With flesh on its bones, the feet of *Dinornis* might have had just the right shape to leave footprints like those found in abundance in the Connecticut Valley.

Hitchcock recalled a day when Owen treated him and his wife to a private viewing

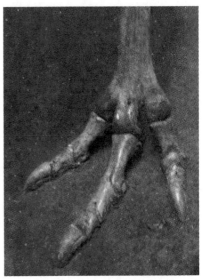

The foot of Dinornis
Copyright©2004 Peabody Museum of Natural
History, Yale University, New Haven, CT

of *Dinornis* during a visit they made to the Hunterian Museum of the Royal College of Surgeons in London in 1850: "He had a room in the Museum," Hitchcock wrote, "and kindly spent an hour or two in showing us its riches. He brought forward the original bone—a fragment of femur only six inches long, from which, by the laws of comparative anatomy, he first constructed and described the Dinornis—the greatest zoological discovery of this present century. His friends warned him not to risk his reputation on so slender a proof of the former existence of this

Richard Owen and a femur, or leg bone, of the extinct bird Dinornis
©*The Natural History Museum, London*

bird, as the mere fragment of a bone; but he had more confidence in the principles of anatomy than in their opinion, and as the result showed, with good reason."

Hitchcock saw Owen's discovery of *Dinornis* as his greatest achievement, even years after his announcement of dinosaurs created a sensation around the world, because it seemed the more significant. Hitchcock had come to form a view of the Connecticut Valley in sandstone time where great birds like *Dinornis* had the run of the place. Bones were irrefutable proof—bone evidence—that extinct birds the size of the "giant ruler" of the Connecticut Valley had once existed.

By the time Hitchcock met Owen in England, he had collected thousands of footprints and was well on his way to describing more than one hundred kinds of bone and trace fossils— from fish to amphibians, reptiles and early crocodiles. Hitchcock believed they were all part of a "great menagerie" of living things that once existed in the valley during the time of the red sandstone. "The records of paleontology lead us to presume that among the animals of oolitic days, to which we now refer as sandstone, we shall find some of very anomalous character," Hitchcock wrote. "The *Ichthyosaurus, Plesiosaurus, Pterodactyle, Iguanodon,* and other huge Saurian reptiles lived then, and from their strangely anomalous characters . . . we ought to presume that the . . . races on this continent would not be less peculiar. And so we find them, judging from their tracks."

Owen's bird discovery shed light on the nature of this ancient world, a feat that surely ranked above his description of dinosaurs. There were then only three dinosaurs—*Megalosaurus, Iguanodon,* and *Hylaeosaurus.* From the looks of these brutish beasts, they had little in common with the "tribes" of ancient birds Hitchcock believed once ran across New Zealand and New England in flocks.

At the same time, Hitchcock recognized that many reptiles had also inhabited the valley. Their presence, even abundance, was also apparent from footprints. He considered them as different from the animals that made the large three-toed tracks. He knew Owen suspected that many bird tracks were actually the tracks of saurian reptiles instead. Neither nor both facts changed Hitchcock's view: "I speak of these animals as certainly birds, though doubts sometimes cross one's mind on this point: and I am aware that with some distinguished zoologists these doubts are strong. But I follow what seems to me at present as the most probable view."

In fact, Hitchcock and Owen were the first to frame a debate still argued in paleontology today: Were birds the descendants of reptiles? Do they exist as sole survivors of the terrible lizards? The link between dinosaurs and birds may have been made sooner if the bones of theropod dinosaurs like those that lived in the Connecticut Valley had been found earlier.

A particularly fascinating clue to whether or not birds are the survivors of dinosaurs was discovered near the end of Hitchcock's life, in 1861, when a remarkably well-preserved specimen of *Archaeopteryx* was found in Germany. *Archaeopteryx* has reptile-like qualities—such as teeth, claws and a long tail—as well as birdlike qualities—like long arms and feathers. Its features helped paleontologists recognize similarities between reptiles and birds, including their feet.

English scientist Thomas Henry Huxley was among the first to propose a connection between birds and dinosaurs based on studies he made of *Archaeopteryx* and the dinosaur *Compsagnathus* early in the 1860s. The discovery of *Archaeopteryx* also helped American Edward Drinker Cope conclude in 1869 that many Connecticut Valley footprints were actually those of dinosaurs. Cope reached his conclusions based in part on evidence provided by *Archaeopteryx* and by bones of *Anchisaurus* which, ironically enough, Hitchcock had described in 1855.

The dinosaur-bird link continues to occupy paleontologists to this day. Former Peabody curator John Ostrom was greatly influenced by a specimen of *Archaeopteryx* he recognized at a museum in the Netherlands in the late 1960s. Jim Farlow has been known to climb into a pen and run alongside ostrich-like birds called rheas for a look at their tracks. Stephen Gatesy has learned

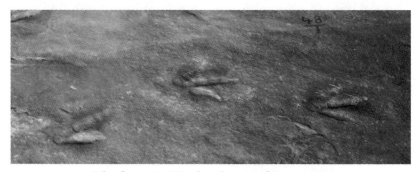

The footprint Hitchcock named Anomoepus
Pratt Museum of Natural History at Amherst College

a great deal about the way living birds walk and made comparisons to reconstruct ways dinosaurs might once have walked. Jacques Gauthier, curator at the Peabody Museum, has revealed how birds are likely the survivors of early meat-eating, theropod dinosaurs.

Ahead of his time?

Hitchcock may have had the wrong idea about which animal it was that made the tracks of his "giant ruler of the valley," but his contributions to paleontology go beyond any single aspect of his work. Almost entirely on his own he came to realize the significance of the tracks not just for what they revealed of the trackmakers, but for what they recounted of the history of the world and the origins of life. He understood the principles of geology—that its processes were immensely slow and that the earth was very old. He recognized that the history of the earth was immensely complex, far more so than could be explained by tales such as the biblical story of the Great Flood.

Hitchcock also saw that there was an order to living things, with some animals being "lower" or "higher" on nature's zoological scale. He described the animal that left its tracks on the slab of *Noah's Raven*, for example, as "low" relative to others he thought related. And he recognized that living things, which once included strange and exotic beasts, had changed over time. "The times have changed," he quoted from a Latin poem, "and the birds must change with them."

In his understanding of the geology of the valley, Hitchcock was without peers. He deduced from its sediments much of what paleontologists like Paul Olsen have since shown to be true. "The probability is that the climate, during the sandstone period, was tropical," Hitchcock wrote, "with perhaps an alternation of wet and dry seasons. The surface, as the gigantic cracks indicate, must have been subject to powerful heat."

Hitchcock realized also that the valley once held large bodies of water and described how these lakes supported large and diverse communities of land-dwelling or terrestrial animals. "The tracks were made on the shores of an estuary, or lake, or river where animals resorted for food, as they now do."

He realized how lakeshore environments could create ideal conditions for preserving the past as trace fossils. Borrowing from Cuvier and Owen, he applied concepts of comparative anatomy to tracks and invented rules for their classification that are still in use today. Questions Hitchcock first asked about whether dinosaurs traveled in groups framed inquiries into behavior for which tracks are now providing intriguing answers.

By the time of his death in 1864, Hitchcock anticipated much about the work that remained to be done, such as studies in climatology (the study of climate changes and trends), sedimentology (the study of sedimentary rocks) and volcanology (the study of volcanoes).

The rub with Deane

Hitchcock never shrank from his critics. Only one ever managed to really get under his skin and that was Dr. Deane of Deerfield, Massachusetts. A few years after Deane first brought his "turkey tracks" to Hitchcock's attention, their relationship soured. Deane claimed he had not been given due credit for the discovery. In fact, Hitchcock always acknowledged Deane's contribution in acquiring the first fossil. Hitchcock also wrote many lengthy explanations for why he felt his own contributions in collecting and studying the fossil could not be denied.

Many paleontologists today can't understand why Hitchcock felt a need to engage in what now seems like such a petty quarrel. His work not only spoke for itself, it had the support of the leading paleontologists of his day, American and English. Given the value of his work and recognition of his peers, Hitchcock's diatribes came off as overly defensive.

It may have been that for Hitchcock, ichnology was about more than science. Although he had long been self-conscious about his lack of a formal education, it may not have been about that either. It may have had to do with the fact that while illness had kept him from accomplishing his dream of going to college, he did not let it keep him from deciphering "nature's hieroglyphics," through sheer force of will. The tracks were his life's work and a personal triumph. He simply may not have wanted to cede to Deane what illness, " … the grand incubus that has lain upon me and oppressed me for fifty years," could not take.

"I am deeply indebted to this science, also, for the enjoyment of my life; I mean physical and intellectual pleasure. He is most conscious of enjoyment from health, who feels it wholly or partially returning to his long debilitated and suffering frame. That feeling have I often experienced as the result of the excursions I have described; or at least the exhilaration thus produced has made me forgetful of my real and fancied ailments, and even expelled the nervousness and gloom of dyspeptic, bronchial, and neuralgic attacks. But it is mainly the intellectual enjoyment of geological research to which I refer. I reckon, and who does not reckon, among the purest pleasures of life, the opportunity to gaze upon the beautiful, the bizarre and the sublime in natural scenery. We never forget them. They have few or no drawbacks, and we enjoy them by retrospection over and over again, and with increasing relish. But though such scenes lie not exclusively with the province of the geologist, he is prepared better than others to enjoy them. His home is among them. There is no mountain so high that he does not scale it, no gulf too profound for his adventurous step, no region so wild and desolate that is not full of interest to him."

—Edward Hitchcock, 1863

The Bone Hunter

Othniel Charles Marsh
"The Bones from the Bridge"
Yale Peabody Museum catalog number YPM 208
Photo Courtesy of the Peabody Museum of Natural History, Yale University, New Haven, CT

"The specimen is part of a skeleton which was probably complete, and in position, when discovered, but for want of proper appreciation at the time, only the posterior [rear] portion was secured."

—O. C. Marsh

It didn't take long for the excitement of having found the rear half of a dinosaur skeleton in a block of brownstone quarried near Manchester, Connecticut, in 1884 to turn to frustration. By the time a search for the front half was begun, it was nowhere to be found. News of the discovery of the rear end—and the loss of the front—reached O. C. Marsh at Yale only after it was too late for him to do anything other than secure the rear end for the museum.

The best guess was that the missing half had been sent, inside an adjacent block quarried earlier, to be laid in the abutments for the nearby Hop Brook Bridge. The block could have been any one of several hundred blocks already laid for the bridge's construction.

It soon became obvious that as long as the bridge remained in service, any thought of reuniting the dinosaur's back half with its front would have to wait. "Professor Marsh tried in vain to locate the block containing the specimen," Lull wrote in his account of the mix-up, "but, when it became evident that little short of the total destruction of the abutments might be necessary, the search was given up and the bridge still has the unique distinction of being the mausoleum of a dinosaur."

As it turned out, it would be 85 years before the bridge was torn down. When it was, one of Marsh's successors, Yale paleontologist and then Peabody curator John Ostrom, would be there waiting.

Marsh & the quarry of Charles O. Wolcott

Marsh wasn't one to let a fossil escape him. As frustrating as it must have been for him to know there were bones sealed inside the Hop Brook Bridge, it turned out there was a bright side to the whole fiasco—and that was the discovery of fossils at the Charles O. Wolcott's Quarry, where the blocks had been cut.

Marsh knew better than anyone what could be found in quarries—with the exception of Edward Drinker Cope. Cope was a great paleontologist in his own right and Marsh's chief rival in the hunt for dinosaurs in the United States in the late 1800s. Indeed, Cope was among the first to declare that many of the Connecticut Valley footprints Hitchcock described were dinosaurian. No account of Marsh's contributions to paleontology would be complete without mention of their rivalry.

Early in their careers, Cope took Marsh to visit some of the quarries in New Jersey where he went to find bones. He later regretted it. Cope eventually accused Marsh of usurping his best contacts among the East Coast quarrymen—just one of many nasty accusations the two flung at each other during their long and acrimonious relationship.

The fossils from the Wolcott Quarry, however, were all Marsh's. After "the Bones from the Bridge" eluded him, Marsh made sure everyone in the quarry kept a sharp eye out for more. By 1891 his patronage paid off. Two more, nearly complete skeletons were dug from the quarry and sent the short distance down the valley to Marsh in New Haven.

The dinosaurs Marsh described from the quarry are known today as *Anchisaurus* or "near lizard," and *Ammosaurus* or "sand lizard," two small, plant-eating dinosaurs once common in the Connecticut Valley and generally regarded as being prosauropods. A recent scientific study by paleontologist Adam Yates has reclassified them as small, primitive sauropods.

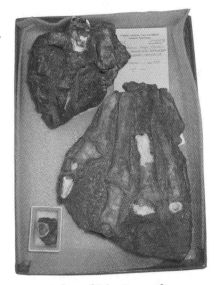

"The new species is represented by perhaps the most perfect Triassic dinosaur yet discovered, as the skull and greater portion of the skeleton were found in place, and in fine preservation," Marsh wrote of *Anchisaurus colurus* in his 1892 description. The skull had been crushed after so long in the ground, but still struck Marsh as

A few of "the Bones from the Bridge" (YPM 208).
Copyright©2004, Peabody Museum of Natural History, Yale University, New Haven, CT

*The skull of a second dinosaur
from the Wolcott Quarry
(YPM 1883).*

Copyright©2004, Peabody Museum of Natural
History, Yale University, New Haven, CT

remarkably "bird-like."

Marsh's description of the third and final skeleton pulled from the quarry, which he named *Anchisaurus solus*, followed soon after. "A fortunate discovery has recently been brought to light, almost the entire skeleton of a diminutive Dinosaur, which may be referred to *Anchisaurus*, but clearly belongs to a different species," Marsh wrote. "It was found in nearly the same horizon [rocks of similar geological age] as the remains above described [*Anchisaurus colurus*], and in the immediate vicinity, so there can be little doubt that it was a contemporary. The skeleton is imbedded in a very coarse matrix [the sand and gravel of hardened sandstone], so difficult to remove that the investigation is only in part complete. The portions uncovered show the animal to have been about three feet in length, and of very delicate proportions. The bones of the skeleton are extremely light and hollow, but most of them are in fair preservation."

The three skeletons found at the Wolcott Quarry, "the Bones from the Bridge" and the two skeletons Marsh received later, earned the quarry distinction as the most productive dinosaur bone site ever excavated in the valley. It retained that title until late June 2003, when the area around the site was paved over to expand the Buckland Hills Mall.

The competitor

O. C. Marsh was born on October 29, 1831, in Lockport, New York. He grew to love the outdoors and was encouraged to pursue his interest in natural history by a local geologist, Colonel Ezekiel Jewett. Jewett introduced Marsh to fossils and minerals during field trips they took together. Marsh's fascination with fossils and minerals grew into a relentless pursuit of relics of the past that continued until the last days of his life.

Marsh proved an astute fossil hunter. During one trip he made to Nova Scotia in 1855, he found a few fossil vertebra, or backbones, which seemed unusual. He studied the bones and several years later, while a student at Yale, showed them to the renowned Harvard paleontologist, Louis Agassiz. Agassiz was so taken by what he saw he sent a note to Benjamin Silliman in 1862 to say the fossil "excited my interest to the highest degree ... we have here undoubtedly a nearer approximation to a synthesis between fish and reptile that has yet been seen."

Never one to be upstaged, Marsh responded to say that Agassiz had not gotten the story entirely right. Marsh designed to set things straight by publishing his own account of the discovery and his description of one of the earliest known reptiles, which he named *Eosaurus acadiansus*, in the very next issue of the *American Journal of Science*.

Bones of a third dinosaur from the Wolcott Quarry (YPM 209).
Copyright©2004, Peabody Museum of Natural History, Yale University, New Haven, CT

The article was an auspicious beginning to a great career and gave a glimpse into Marsh's seemingly insatiable competitiveness. His ambition would later be rivaled only by the size and number of astonishingly bizarre animals that he and his field workers pulled from the ground in the last few decades of the nineteenth century.

Marsh was also privileged in life to have had a wealthy uncle, George Peabody, who indulged his interest in science. Peabody was a merchant and financier who amassed great wealth and became one of the first great philanthropists in American history. Marsh's mother, who died before he was three, was Peabody's younger sister. Peabody looked out for his nephew financially after his sister's death. Peabody paid Marsh's tuition at Yale and financed his postgraduate training in Europe. Peabody left Marsh a substantial inheritance after his death in 1869.

Peabody made sizable donations to numerous other educational institutions in the United States and to housing the poor of England, his adopted home. He was honored for his philanthropy by Queen Victoria.

Peabody saw to it that Marsh had the means to collect his fossils and a grand edifice in which to house them. Marsh made the most of the advantages he was given and went on to make many sensational contributions to paleontology. Specimens he collected and those collected for him continue to play an invaluable role in advancing knowledge in the field today. An odd quirk of history is the fact that Marsh was actually opposed to mounting fossils for display. Only a papier-mache model based on a temporarily mounted mammal skeleton was ever mounted during Marsh's era— and that was for a World Fair exhibit.

The bone rush

Marsh's zeal for obtaining fossils for the Peabody Museum was both his great strength and greatest weakness. For all his accomplishments, as enormous as they were—literally—he seems doomed to be remembered as much for his foibles, especially the imbroglio with Cope.

"Marsh discovered just how diverse dinosaurs really were," says Jim Farlow. "He and Cope were very bad boys, but they sure found an awful lot of dinosaurs and opened our eyes to the range of body forms and the sheer exuberance of species of dinosaurs. I would say that's probably his greatest contribution from the standpoint of dinosaur paleontology—that and giving us a role model of what not to do."

Field crews working for Marsh and Cope (along with other noted collectors such as Barnum Brown who collected for the American Museum of Natural History in New York City) helped ignite a period of dinosaur fossil collecting that has never been equaled and has since become notorious as "the bone rush" of the 1870s to the 1890s. Theirs were among the first expeditions to search the American West for bones since William Clark reported in his journal what he thought was a three-foot-long "rib of a fish." Clark made his find near what is now Billings, Montana, while on expedition with Meriwether Lewis in 1806.

Like Clark and paleontologist Ferdinand Hayden, who explored the West in the 1850s, the bone hunters were all adventurers. In photographs taken of the Yale expeditions he led to the American West in the early 1870s, Marsh and his students looked more like gangs of gun-toting desperados than paleontologists. In those days, the West was still very wild. Firearms were kept within arms reach, but Marsh was undeterred by hardship or danger in his pursuit of fossils.

Marsh mounted four expeditions to the West in the early 1870s and later hired crews to collect fossils for the Peabody

The Yale College Scientific Expedition of 1872
Courtesy of the Peabody Museum of Natural History, Yale University, New Haven, CT

Museum. There were soon so many sites to work and so many bones to excavate that Marsh kept teams of workers busy year-round at dig sites at Morrison and Canon City, Colorado, and at Como Bluff, Wyoming. Marsh relied on a trusted few to handle field operations, including several men with Connecticut roots. Benjamin Mudge was a graduate of Wesleyan University in Middletown. Samuel Williston earned his medical degree and Ph.D. from Yale. William Reed was born near Hartford and later worked for the Union Pacific Railroad in Wyoming as foreman of Como Station. Reed became fascinated with dinosaurs after discovering several bones while hunting antelope. He and station agent William Carlin sent word of the finds to Marsh, who hired the men to dig fossils for the museum.

The bone rush resulted in thousands of crates filled with bones being shipped back to New Haven for Marsh. Among them were skeletons of the giant dinosaurs that have dominated the popular imagination ever since, such as *Apatosaurus* (*"Brontosaurus"*), *Stegosaurus* and *Triceratops*. As sensational as Hitchcock's descriptions of fossil footprints and Owen's descriptions of the first few dinosaurs had been, the fossils Marsh described were in a league of their own. Looking at them in the Peabody Museum today, it is still hard to imagine how a world filled with such creatures ever existed.

Marsh's legacy

It is difficult to stand in the Great Hall of the Peabody Museum and not see the fossils collected for and named by Marsh as his most enduring legacy. The skeleton Marsh's teams collected of *Apatosaurus*, the great plant-eater that stood many times taller than a human and grew to be over 80 feet long, remains the centerpiece of the Great Hall. Nearby is *Stegosaurus*, the bizarre-looking dinosaur famous for its spiked tail and the two rows of bony plates that lined its back. It was mounted using bits of the skeletons of several different individuals that Marsh's men collected for him. There are also three skulls of *Triceratops* with its huge frill and intimidating horns on display in the hall.

These giants are among the more than 70 species of dinosaurs Marsh described. He proposed a system for classifying dinosaurs into four groups: theropods, ornithopods, sauropods, and stegosaurs. Systems for classifying the dinosaurs have been refined and redefined a great deal since, but many paleontologists still refer to dinosaurs as belonging to one or another of the groups first proposed by Marsh and known today as sub-orders.

Marsh also pioneered techniques for making skeletal reconstructions of dinosaurs, drawings of their skeletons as they had once fit together. He published reconstructions of *Apatosaurus*, *Stegosaurus*, *Triceratops*, the Connecticut Valley specimens of *Anchisaurus* and several other fossil vertebrates based on their bones.

While Marsh may be best known for his dinosaurs, there was

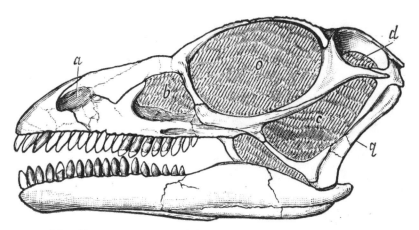

*Marsh's reconstruction of the skull of Anchisaurus, known
from the Wolcott Quarry in Manchester, Connecticut.*
Courtesy, Connecticut Department of Environmental Protection

never a fossil he didn't want to study. In fact, he studied fossils of all sorts and made many contributions to the knowledge of living things beyond just dinosaurs.

Marsh also studied early mammals from carnivores to primates. He is known for his studies on the evolution of horses and for two groups of large, knob-headed mammals called the Dinocerata and brontotheres. He named many new flying reptiles, pterosaurs, and swimming reptiles, including those known as mosasaurs.

Marsh helped advance the knowledge of the link between reptiles and birds with his description of "birds with teeth," including *Hesperornis* and *Ichthyornis*.

Marsh presented his entire collection to Yale in 1898, the year before his death. After complaining of feeling ill, he left his lab for the last time in March 1899 with the help of his fossil preparator, Hugh Gibb. He died of pneumonia days later, on March 18, 1899.

As much as Benjamin Silliman and Edward Hitchcock did to establish the tradition of dinosaur science in the Connecticut Valley, it was O. C. Marsh, his uncle George Peabody, and raw ambition that guaranteed its continuance.

63

The Teacher

Richard Swann Lull

Photo Courtesy of the Peabody Museum of Natural History, Yale University, New Haven, CT

> *"After the exhaustive researches of the late Edward Hitchcock, workers [were] attracted to other more productive fields leaving the footprints aside as relics of little moment compared with the wonderful discoveries in the great unknown west ... Little was done from the time of the publication of Edward Hitchcock's notable 'Ichnology of New England' ... until 1904, when a new study of the tracks in the light of recent paleontology was published."*
>
> —Richard Swann Lull

That study was Lull's own. After the frenzy of Marsh's bone rush, there was time to look back on what had been accomplished in the Connecticut Valley since the time Pliny Moody found *Noah's Raven*. Just as Marsh was a man for his time, Lull was well suited to the tasks that remained unfinished at the beginning of the twentieth century.

Richard Lull became interested in the Connecticut Valley footprints in 1894 while an assistant professor of zoology at the Massachusetts State Agricultural College, now the University of Massachusetts at Amherst. The State College was just a short distance down what is today Route 9 from Amherst College and Edward Hitchcock's magnificent collection of fossil footprints.

Hitchcock's collection had by then become neglected and was in need of restudy. Lull realized that paleontology and the knowledge of dinosaurs had progressed a great deal since Hitchcock's death in 1864, and consequently became interested in updating Hitchcock's work to reflect contemporary science. "Whether or not birds were present is a mooted question," he later wrote. " ... Hitchcock considered all the birdlike tracks to have been of avian origin [the term "avian" was originally coined by Owen to describe the birdlike characteristics of footprints discovered by Hitchcock], but the discovery of dinosaurian remains soon swung popular if not scientific opinion to the opposite extreme, and all the tracks were believed to have been made by dinosaurs. I believe, in most instances, this group of footprints is demonstrably dinosaurian."

Lull found the work of the footprints intriguing and the conditions of museum research more to his liking. Lull would later go on several expeditions to the West, including a dig in 1899 that recovered the skeleton of *Apatosaurus* displayed at the American Museum of Natural History in New York City and several others as curator at the Peabody, but fieldwork didn't hold the same appeal. Lull's eyesight had been poor since he was a child and the routine of examining fossils under laboratory conditions proved more to his taste. According to a biographer, G. G. Simpson, Lull often remarked that the best collecting he knew was in the basement of the Peabody Museum.

Lull's first study of Hitchcock's material formed the basis of his Ph.D. thesis at Columbia University and was completed in 1903.

He published several subsequent updates after becoming assistant professor of paleontology at Yale and associate curator at the Peabody in 1906, including a major work in 1915. "The purpose of the *1915 Bulletin*," he wrote, "was to restore the environment, both physiographic and climatic, to clothe it with its proper vegetation and to discuss fully as may be the animal life of that distant day."

Lull's final report on the subject, *Triassic Life of the Connecticut Valley*, was published in 1953 by the State Geological and Natural History Survey of Connecticut. The last revision included new ideas, notably a theory developed by professor Paul Krynine that "a hot and humid climate with an abundance of rain" had existed in the valley. Krynine's ideas anticipate current conceptions of the climate early in the age of dinosaurs.

"The profusion of species of animals represented by the tracks, which of course include the creatures the skeletons of which are known, seems to be as great if not greater than that of any other known vertebrate fauna of prehistoric times," Lull concluded in his 1953 report, "and emphasizes once more the usual incompleteness of our geological record and the countless multitude of creatures which peopled our globe in the more remote ages."

Lull's models of dinosaurs he thought made the track Sauropus barratti.
Pratt Museum of Natural History at Amherst College

Triassic Life of the Connecticut Valley remains a classic. "It's had a huge influence on me," says Paul Olsen. His copy is worn and dog-eared, but with its binding intact. "When I was a boy I got involved with finding footprints; this was the classic work for the study of footprints and, actually, still remains today the most authoritative text."

Time, June 1, 1925
Courtesy, Paul E. Olsen

Accomplishments

Richard Swann Lull was born on November 6, 1867, in Annapolis, Maryland. He spent most of his professional life in service to dinosaur science, organic evolution, Yale and the Peabody Museum. Like Silliman, Lull was a dignified and esteemed teacher. His classes were among the most popular taught at Yale. At the height of their popularity, his classes exceeded 400 students a year, according to one of his successors at Yale, Joseph Gregory.

Lull also devoted a great deal of effort to dinosaur restoration and exhibition. Unlike Marsh, who had skeletal reconstructions done, Lull fully restored extinct animals in the form of models. He fashioned small-scale models of local dinosaurs known from bones, such as *Anchisaurus*. His idea was to show the animal fully fleshed out on one side with a cutaway view of its skeleton on the other.

Lull also had drawings made from his scale models to present his vision for how the trackmakers of the Connecticut Valley may have appeared. Among these was a sketch of a prosauropod like one Lull thought made the footprint *Otozoum moodii*, found at the

Moody family farm. Lull was among the first to link this footprint to prosauropod dinosaurs.

Also unlike Marsh, Lull had fossil specimens mounted for public display. The present Peabody Museum building opened while Lull was director. He saw to it that the bones of many of the animals Marsh had reconstructed as drawings were actually erected. These amazing and enormous displays can be seen in the Great Hall today. The sheer size and weight of the bones made this a monumental task. It required complex arrangements of iron supports to hold the hundreds of bones together.

Richard Swann Lull served Yale for nearly fifty years. He retired from Yale as Sterling Professor (Yale's highest rank) in 1936, and as Director of the Peabody Museum in 1938, but remained active into his eighties. He served as editor of the *American Journal of Science* until 1949. He died on April 22, 1957, at the age of 89.

The Visionary
John Ostrom
"The Bones from the Bridge"
Yale Peabody Museum catalog number YPM 208 (continued 85 years later)
Photo: Peter Galton. Courtesy of the Peabody Museum of Natural History, Yale University, New Haven, CT

> *"Unfortunately for Marsh, the front half of the skeleton was missing. Presumably it was embedded in the adjacent block of sandstone that had been hauled away to the construction. . . A search was made for the missing block, to no avail, and ever since 1884 Curators of ... the Peabody Museum have kept a hopeful eye on the brownstone bridge in Manchester—waiting for its demolition."*

> —John Ostrom

The long wait to reunite "the Bones from the Bridge" came to an end in August 1969. When at last the Hop Brook Bridge was scheduled for demolition, Ostrom and state officials carefully took it apart, block by block, and searched for fossils.

Their careful labor paid off. "The bridge came tumbling

down," Ostrom wrote, "nudged by a D-8 bulldozer and a clam shell suspended from an 80-foot crane ... The State Highway authorities arranged for our use of heavy equipment and permitted me to supervise the demolition of the bridge. Some 400 sandstone blocks were examined during the two-day project, and two were found that contained fossil bone. One shows several ribs and the other contains part of a femur or thighbone. The latter almost certainly is part of the femur missing from the original specimen of *Ammosaurus*. The ribs in the other block may belong to the same animal or be part of another individual. How much of the missing parts were recovered will not be known for some time . . . After 85 years a few more months won't matter."

The two blocks were taken back to Yale. The back half of Marsh's "sand lizard," which was partially complete, was reunited with its front half. Both remain preserved today in the Peabody Museum's vertebrate paleontology collection.

Life, dinosaurs, birds & *Deinonychus*

John Ostrom was at the Hop Brook Bridge that summer day in 1969 because of all he knew about the generations of paleontologists who preceded him in the Connecticut Valley and at Yale. He understood his responsibility to carry on their work—and was there to finish what Marsh had started.

Where else in the world but in the Connecticut Valley did paleontologists carry on such a tradition? What institution but the Peabody Museum would have stood watch over that bridge for so long? And where else would one of the most renowned paleontologists of his day be sending hand signals to a bulldozer operator in a search for fossils left behind by the man who held his position nearly a century before?

Ostrom understood all those things, and yet made his mark by constantly questioning past assumptions and long held beliefs. He breathed life into fossils. Where many viewed dinosaurs as lumbering, cold-blooded and stupid, Ostrom's discoveries indicated

John Ostrom
Courtesy of the Peabody Museum of Natural
History, Yale University, New Haven, CT

that at least some may have been cunningly dangerous, warm-blooded and as agile as acrobats. He looked for clues to their behavior in their anatomy, in the arrangements of their fossilized remains, and in Connecticut Valley trackways.

Like Silliman, Hitchcock, Marsh and Lull, Ostrom was also a man for his time. Dinosaur science had grown old and musty in the century and a half since Pliny Moody dug up *Noah's Raven*. It needed new blood, new spark and a new leader—someone who could bring new ideas and new energy. Ostrom was that person.

"He created an environment at Yale in the 1960s and 1970s where you thought about dinosaurs as living animals," says Jim Farlow, one of Ostrom's former students. "I mean that was the most exciting place in the world to be if you were interested in such questions. Yale was an amazingly stimulating place under John Ostrom. He created an environment where it was just so exciting to be working on dinosaurs. A lot of my own research on various aspects of dinosaur biology couldn't have been done anywhere other than at Yale."

Changing perceptions

One of Ostrom's greatest discoveries came near the end of his 1964 field season at the now famous "Shrine site" in the Cloverly Formation of south central Montana. The few bones he found on one last walk through the area turned out to be the tip of an iceberg that held the remains of at least four small, meat-eating, theropod dinosaurs and pieces of a large plant-eater.

"It was finding *Deinonychus* and looking at its functional morphology that led him to say this is not a sluggish animal—there's more to these guys than just the image of dim-witted brutes slurping their way through swamps," Jim says.

Based on the way their bones were found in association with those of the larger plant-eater, Ostrom proposed that the theropods—a particularly nasty sort, well armed with ripping claws—hunted in packs like modern-day wolves. He named the theropod *Deinonychus*, or "terrible claw" for the large, sickle-shaped claw on the second toe of its hind feet. He also noted the unique design of the tail, which they held out straight behind them like the balancing poles acrobats use to perform high-wire acts. Its anatomy suggested *Deinonychus* was capable of leaping at its prey, grabbing hold with its long forearms and finishing things off with the large, eagle-like talons on its hind feet.

The unfortunate victim at the Shrine site, a plant-eater Ostrom named *Tenontosaurus*, may have succeeded at fighting off or killing several of the vicious theropods, but apparently could not beat off the entire pack. It weighed thousands of pounds perhaps—enough, Ostrom suspected, to do considerable damage as it swatted or fell on the much smaller and lighter *Deinonychus*.

To Ostrom's mind, the Shrine site discovery was evidence that dinosaurs were swift, agile and intelligent enough to cooperate with others like themselves to bring down large prey. While Ostrom's ideas remain provocative, there is little doubt that the vision he had of living dinosaurs has gone a long way toward changing people's perceptions of them ever since.

Tweet, tweet!

"The other thing I think John will be remembered for will be, you know, 'tweet, tweet!'" Jim Farlow says. "He resurrected and made respectable the idea that birds are derived from theropod dinosaurs. It's now the consensus view among the majority of paleontologists; I even think it's true of ornithologists now."

Ostrom drew a connection between theropods and birds after happening upon another fossil, one that struck him as remarkably similar to *Deinonychus* in many ways. After finishing his work on the animals of the Cloverly Formation, he had begun a study of flying reptiles, or pterosaurs, and was in the Netherlands examining the fossil collection of a local museum. A small specimen from Germany identified as a flying reptile looked to Ostrom more like a small theropod dinosaur. Holding it to the light he saw what looked like feathers and knew instantly it was actually a previously unrecognized specimen of *Archaeopteryx*, the earliest known bird and only the fourth specimen identified up to that point.

The similarities between *Deinonychus*, the small theropod he'd

Courtesy of the Peabody Museum of Natural History, Yale University, New Haven, CT

found in Montana, and the fossil of *Archaeopteryx* found in Germany, were fascinating. They led Ostrom to begin an important new study of the possible link between dinosaurs and birds.

In a series of papers written in the mid-1970s, including a report published in 1976 entitled *"Archaeopteryx and the Origin of Birds,"* Ostrom clearly demonstrated that *Deinonychus* and other closely-related, small theropods with grabbing hands shared unique features with *Archaeopteryx*. This group of theropods was later named the "Maniraptora" by Jacques

73

Gauthier, Ostrom's successor at the Peabody Museum.

In so doing, Ostrom resurrected an earlier, previously dismissed hypothesis that birds originated from dinosaurs. He established that birds evolved from a group of small meat-eating dinosaurs (the maniraptorans) such as *Deinonychus*.

"Not everybody buys it," Jim Farlow observes, "but most believe that it's the most plausible explanation. The paper he published was, in my opinion, the single most influential statement of the case."

More than a century after Edward Hitchcock and Richard Owen first encountered similarities between reptiles and birds, Ostrom made the first convincing statement of the case for a theropod ancestry of birds. Ostrom's hypothesis has been supported by many different researchers, including Jacques Gauthier. Using a modern approach to comparative anatomy and classification known as cladistics, in 1986 Jacques Gauthier presented detailed evidence to show that theropod dinosaurs never really went extinct. Instead, they survive today as birds.

Jacques and his former student Alan Gishlick have been looking into the evolution and function of maniraptoran forelimbs. They have their own ideas about the evolution of flight. It's possible, they think, that the way early maniraptorans used their forelimbs to seize and clamp down on prey may have paved the way for later dinosaur forms to fly by flapping wings. Movements that theropods like *Deinonychus* made with their forelimbs to take prey may have been the precursors to the flight stroke in birds.

Paved paradise and put up a parking lot

Once the most productive dinosaur bone site in New England, people now come to the Charles O. Wolcott Quarry to look for bargains. Much of the area around the quarry, where most of the valley's best dinosaur skeletons were collected in the 1880s and 1890s, including "the Bones from the Bridge," has since been paved over for parking at the Buckland Hills Mall.

Were there other dinosaur bones waiting to be found? If there were, some may been ground into aggregate along with the 300,000 cubic yards of Connecticut Valley brownstone that was dug out to make way for the expansion of the shopping center during the summer of 2000—a little over a century after the first bones from the site were built into the Hop Brook Bridge.

Tons of brownstone had been blown to bits by the time John Ostrom, then retired, was allowed on the site. "I was one very unhappy man," he told *The Hartford Courant*. Where he had succeeded in finding long-lost fossils during the demolition of the Hop Brook Bridge, Ostrom found nothing here as construction workers laid waste to the area around the old Wolcott Quarry. "Sid Quarrier, then a geologist for the state … said he and other workers were forbidden from helping Ostrom inspect the construction because the contractor deemed the state's insurance insufficient," *The Courant* reported. "Poor Connecticut," Ostrom told the newspaper.

Unlike the Hop Brook Bridge, it isn't likely much will be found at the site after the mall is knocked down—and it probably won't last 85 years. If fossil fragments remain, they're likely specks in the pavement.

The mall is an example of one big difference in doing geology or paleontology fieldwork in the valley today as opposed to centuries ago. In Edward Hitchcock's day, life in Connecticut and Massachusetts was centered around small farms. The land was kept clear by grazing sheep and dairy cows, or by the planting and harvesting of crops. With trees cleared for farming and no large buildings, geological features were often plainly apparent. Geologists could stand on high ground and get a quick impression of landforms for miles around. Rivers were uncontrolled, and periodic flooding often exposed fossil sites along their banks. Paleontologists could get access to sites simply by asking for permission from a local farmer or landowner.

Today, large human populations exert greater pressure on natural resources and open space. Modern society uses resources differently. There are fewer farms. Tracts of new homes have been built. More trees are allowed to grow. Commercial development—malls, factories and corporate parks—expanded into areas that were unused before. Interstates have been built and floodgates added to control rivers. Part of the challenge for future science in the Connecticut Valley will be preserving sites that hold clues to the past.

The Seeker
Paul Olsen
Extinctions & the ecological expansion of the dinosaurs

Paul Olsen is trying to make a point when he stops and spins in his chair and begins searching his computer for an example of what he's talking about. He scrolls through one of the lectures he delivers as part of the class he teaches at Columbia University in New York City on dinosaurs and the history of life, until the image of a large reptile of improbable proportions comes up on his screen.

It's not what Olsen the professor is looking for, but the kid who grew up loving fossils can't resist. He clicks on the image to play a QuickTime clip of the beast and a grin spreads over his face. "That's *Postosuchus*, one of the top carnivores in the Triassic," he says, spreading his hands wide apart. "It could have a head this big!"

As much as he has learned about prehistoric reptiles since he began hunting for fossils as a teenager, it's his fascination with the brutes that motivates him. Paul's enthusiasm is bolstered by having identified a nearly complete skeleton of a predator like *Postosuchus* himself once—and a very hungry one at that. In its stomach Paul and his colleagues found two smaller reptiles, a toe from a third,

A rendering of the super-continent Pangaea by Paul E. Olsen
Courtesy, Paul E. Olsen

and part of an amphibian. Crushed beneath all was an early form of crocodile with a bite missing from its neck, suggesting the two died in mortal combat. Phytosaur teeth found scattered around hinted that yet another primitive, crocodile-like reptile made a meal of the combatants after their struggle ended.

The animation ends and Paul picks up where he left off, describing an environmental disaster he says left its mark in the Connecticut Valley 201 million years ago—at about the same time dinosaurs first began to grow large and diverse. "It was a mass extinction," Paul says, "one that's highly controversial right now. This extinction resulted in a change of course in the history of life—and one that is at least partially responsible for why we are here today." Paul's theory about this extinction, which he believes occurred at the boundary between the end of the Triassic Period of time and the beginning of the Jurassic Period, has put the Connecticut Valley back in paleontology's spotlight once again.

Paul has been studying the geology and paleontology of the valley and the rift basins of eastern North America for decades, from the time he was in high school and throughout his undergraduate and graduate studies at Yale. What he's found in local sandstones and siltstones has provoked a new debate over how dinosaurs got started down their path to success, and just when they grew to dominate life on earth.

Paul believes the age of dinosaurs began much the way it ended—with a global, environmental disaster caused by a meteor that crashed into the earth 201 million years ago. The disaster devastated life in the seas and, by the time the dust settled, wiped out half the animal families that had existed on land. Those that survived inherited the world. The extinction brought an end to many primitive reptiles, including *Postosuchus*, but gave others a new start. The newer models, especially dinosaurs, got just the sort of opportunity they needed to grow and expand.

The story is just one of many in a long history of life that extends far back into the ancient past. The history of the earth reaches even further—to a vast, practically unknowable span of time during which the planet was an empty place and devoid of life—to what geologists know as the deep past of geologic time.

Geologic Time in the Valley 5

The view from atop the traprock ridges at Castle Craig
Photo: Nancy McHone

T he trick to telling any story is to make sure all the parts
are in place. Any good tale answers to the same few basic
questions, often right at the beginning. It reveals who
is involved, what they're up to, how they came to be, and where
and when the story takes place. All it takes is for any one of these
details to be left out and the thread of a story can be lost.

Science is no different. It's not enough to know what the
events of the past were—or even how they came to pass. What
is often essential is to know when things happened. The great
challenge of geology has always been to get a hold on time and to
know, as precisely as possible, just when the most significant events
in the history of the earth occurred.

Before scientists formulated a concept about the age of the
earth, or geologic time, and the pace of change over its 4.6 billion-
year history, what was learned of mountains and valleys and the
rocks underlying them was of little use.

Early efforts to understand the ages of the earth, or geologic time, showed the problem had a couple of parts. There was relative time, the age of different rocks as measured against others nearby, and there was absolute time, the age of rocks against some sort of measure, such as years. Relative time was easier to judge than absolute time. Even before the age of the earth was well understood it was possible to look at rocks together and recognize which were older and which were younger.

The concept of relative time was explored by the Danish philosopher Nicholas Steno in the late 1600s and the Scottish geologist James Hutton in the late 1700s. Looking at layers of rock, or strata, they realized that individual layers represented different periods in geologic time. Theoretically, the layers near the bottom of the pile were put down first and were relatively older. Upper layers were added later and were relatively younger. The concept is known today as the principle of superposition.

William Smith advanced the search for a measure of absolute time early in the 1800s. Smith was an engineer by trade and an amateur fossil hunter by avocation. His work digging canals allowed him to do both. He came to know not only the layers of bedrock underlying much of the British Isles, but the fossils associated with them. Smith realized that the oldest rocks contained no evidence of fossils. Middle-aged rocks contained fossils of sea life, while still younger strata contained fossils of life on land.

Smith published his findings in the form of a map of the geology of the British Isles in 1815. His map organized rocks in chronological order according to the fossils associated with them, for the first time. Where the principle of superposition of strata made it possible to judge the relative age of rocks within connected areas, Smith's map provided a system for placing rocks from separate locations on an absolute timescale.

He used the fact that fossils, unlike rocks, are limited in

their occurrence to discrete periods of time. The fact that various animals appeared at certain times in the past and later disappeared or went extinct is unchanging. Wherever fossils were found, they provided a natural order that could be used to place the rocks associated with them in time. "Once dinosaurs die out, they can never return again," paleontologist Stephen Jay Gould once pointed out, "whereas quartz can be formed at any time."

The geologic column

Smith's map plotted the first section of a timescale for the ages of the earth. His work led to the ages of the earth eventually being plotted on timescales in years, known today as the geologic column, and to a new field known as biostratigraphy.

The work Smith started still goes on today. Many paleontologists, like Spencer Lucas, continue to work to correlate or define relationships between fossil records around the world. International commissions have also been convened to integrate new findings and set standards for a global chronostratigraphic timescale.

The greatest division of earth time, nearly four billion years, is Precambrian time. This time stretches back to when the earth first coalesced and includes many significant milestones that followed. The earth's crust cooled during Precambrian time, the atmosphere went from being highly toxic to oxygen rich, living cells appeared, and the first multicellular animals evolved. Periods of time since the Precambrian have been comparatively brief. They mark many geological milestones, but are defined as much by milestones in the evolution of life which have occurred since early living systems first appeared. The Paleozoic Era refers to a time of primitive life, the Mesozoic Era to a time of middle life and the Cenozoic Era, which we inhabit today, refers to recent life.

The age of dinosaurs seems as if it was a long time ago, but when considered on the scale of earth time, events of the past few hundred million years are instead shown to be relatively recent. As ancient as dinosaurs appear to us, the fact is that when dinosaurs first appeared they represented the pinnacle of evolutionary progress—the culmination of billions of years of change and adaptation.

Just as dinosaurs were preceded by a long series of evolutionary changes, the region we know today as Connecticut was preceded by long series of geological changes. The earth was more than three billion years old before the rocks that exist in the state today were formed. The geologic history of Connecticut goes back perhaps 1.4 billion years, to an ancestral continent known as Proto-North America. Much of the state formed later, in a series of continental collisions between 1.1 billion and 250 million years ago.

The Connecticut Valley was formed during the Mesozoic Era which began some 250 million years ago. All the world's continents were then pressed into one vast landmass to form the super-continent of Pangaea. The first dinosaurs appeared not long after, about 230 or 225 million years ago. Modern plants, such as flowers and grasses, and animals, such as birds and mammals, also appeared in Mesozoic time, along with giant insects.

The glaciers which shaped much of modern Connecticut during the last Ice Age receded as recently as 15,000 years ago and native people arrived not long after. Much of the local landscape and modern features, such as Long Island Sound, have existed only since the ice melted.

Most of what is known of geology and paleontology has been learned in just the past few centuries. Perhaps the most significant developments have come since the concept of deep time was formed. The geologic column on the opposite page gives an overview of geological and evolutionary events in the history of Connecticut. The following pages include contributions by geologist Greg McHone and highlight events in the history of the earth leading up to and following the time when dinosaur fossils were preserved in the Connecticut Valley.

The Geologic History of Connecticut

Years in Millions	Eon	Era	Period	Epoch	Geological & Evolutionary Events
0.011			Quaternary	Holocene	Humans arrive
1.8			Quaternary	Pleistocene	Dramatic changes in climate; **Ice sheets** cover & uncover CT
5		Cenozoic	Tertiary	Pliocene	Marine coastal sedimentation
23		Cenozoic	Tertiary	Miocene	Erosional interval
38		Cenozoic	Tertiary	Oligocene	Erosional interval
54		Cenozoic	Tertiary	Eocene	Semi-tropical plants in Vermont
66		Cenozoic	Tertiary	Paleocene	Erosional interval; **Mammals expand**
146	Phanerozoic	Mesozoic	Cretaceous		Shallow sea covers coastal New England; Uplift & erosion inland; **Birds expand**
201	Phanerozoic	Mesozoic	Jurassic		Atlantic Ocean opens, south flowing rivers (Ct., Thames, etc.) develop; Climate grows wetter; CAMP Lava flows; **Dinosaurs expand**
250	Phanerozoic	Mesozoic	Triassic		Rifting of Pangaea begins; sedimentation of Hartford basin; SW rivers flow in semi-arid climate; **Primitive dinosaurs appear**
286	Phanerozoic	Paleozoic	Permian		**Pangaea completed; Alleghenian Orogeny:** Alleghenian mountain building; Stony Creek granites, eastern pegmatites
325	Phanerozoic	Paleozoic	Pennsylvanian		Coals deposited in coastal swamps; Alleghenian Orogeny begins
360	Phanerozoic	Paleozoic	Mississipian		Passive margin sedimentation
410	Phanerozoic	Paleozoic	Devonian		**Acadian Orogeny:** Sedimentation in eastern CT, granites, western pegmatites melted by burial, others metamorphosed; **Early amphibians**
440	Phanerozoic	Paleozoic	Silurian		Taconic highlands eroded; Land plants
505	Phanerozoic	Paleozoic	Ordovician		**Taconic Orogeny:** marine muds & sands buried and metamorphosed
544	Phanerozoic	Paleozoic	Cambrian		**Cambrian Explosion**; Fossils seashells; Carbonate depositions on passive margin
650	Precambrian		Neoproterozoic		600-550: Late phase Iapetan rifting
	Precambrian		Neoproterozoic		750-700: Early phases Iapetan rifting
900	Precambrian		Neoproterozoic		
	Precambrian		Mesoproterozoic		**Grenvillian Orogeny** (1,100-950)
	Precambrian		Mesoproterozoic		**Oldest rocks** in Connecticut
1,600	Precambrian		Mesoproterozoic		
	Precambrian		Paleoproterozoic		Atmospheric oxygen increases
2,500	Precambrian		Paleoproterozoic		

4.6 billion years (Precambrian)

The earth, along with the other planets and the sun, coalesces from a large cloud of gas and dust that form the solar system. Our present moon splits off from the early earth within a few hundred million years, perhaps from a planetary collision.

4 billion years (Precambrian)

Less dense rocks of the earth's crust separate from the heavier mantle and iron core. The surface cools enough for the atmosphere to stabilize and for water to condense from steam from volcanoes. Unlike most planets, earth's volcanoes continue to produce gases that enrich our atmosphere and allow plants to flourish.

3.8 billion years (Precambrian)

Life appears, indicated by a "light carbon" isotope in the oldest sedimentary rocks known (from Greenland). Fossils were not well preserved, but tiny spherical marks may be from bacteria. The air is rich in nitrogen (N) and carbon dioxide (CO_2) with some methane, water vapor and other gases, but very little oxygen (O_2) is present.

3.5 billion years (Precambrian)

Layers of simple bacteria and algae-like cells work together to form the stromatolites (dome-shaped structures) in shallow warm ocean muds. Fossils formed from stromatolites in Australia survive as the oldest known.

2 billion years (Precambrian)

There are signs, such as oxidized iron minerals that collect in sedimentary layers, that O_2 is becoming more abundant in the atmosphere. Eukaryotes (cells with a membrane-bound nucleus, the ancestors of all animals) appear.

1.4 billion years (Precambrian)

The oldest rocks in Connecticut, in the southwestern area of the state, recrystallize from even older rocks during a collision of tectonic plates called the Grenville Orogeny. These are similar to metamorphic rocks in Vermont and New York that today lie beneath sedimentary layers of Proto-North America.

1 billion years (Precambrian)

Photosynthesizing organisms (algae and plankton) thrive in shallow seas. These plants metabolize CO_2 and release O_2 into the air as a by-product. The Grenville Orogeny is ending in eastern Proto-North America, which includes westernmost Connecticut. The super-continent of Rodinia forms and dominates the map of the world for the next 400 million years.

600 million years ago (Precambrian)

Marine photosynthesizing organisms remove so much CO_2 from the air that the climate becomes very cold, causing a massive "snowball earth" ice age. Tropical oceans are frozen beneath a mile of sea ice. Volcanic activity eventually renews CO_2 and the earth swings wildly back, to a hot, ice-free climate. Rodinia breaks into several large continents. Simple marine animals, without hard parts, become larger and very diverse. Rocks of eastern Connecticut, known as the Avalon Terrane, form in a volcanic zone along the western margin of Gondwanaland, one of the large continents that are moving away from Proto-North America.

545 million years (Cambrian)

The "Cambrian Explosion" of marine animals is recorded by fossils of a huge variety of animals, including corals and sponges, worms, clams, arthropods, etc. Many animals inhabit the shallow, calcareous-mud bottom of warm shallow oceans along the edges of the continents, including westernmost Connecticut. Early fish appear, the ancestors of all modern vertebrates (animals with backbones) appear late in Cambrian time.

480 million years (Ordovician)

A mass extinction of unknown cause marks the end of the Ordovician. Western Connecticut rises as ocean volcanic rocks are pushed into the ancient continent during the Taconic Orogeny.

The eastern two-thirds of the state remain under an ancient ocean called Iapetos.

425 million years (Silurian)

Simple wetland and shoreline plants colonize the land. Scorpions and other arthropods also move onto the land, aided by oxygen levels in the air now above ten percent.

395 million years (Devonian)

The first vascular plants (plants with specialized structures that conduct fluids and add structural strength) appear. Ferns, reeds and horsetails rapidly evolve. Land-dwelling insects grow common. The first amphibians evolve from lobe-finned fish. They are able to breathe air and crawl on land, but return to the water to lay eggs. The Iapetos Ocean is destroyed as its crust is pushed into the continent (the Acadian Orogeny), causing the sea floor muds to metamorphose into gneiss and schist. Granites rising in the crust of west-central Connecticut melt. Volcanic island arcs and distinct regions of the Iapetos Ocean form the geologic zones of New England known as terranes. At the end of the Devonian, an extinction eliminates about half of all the world's living species.

330 million years (Carboniferous)

Tall coniferous trees appear. Large flying insects (dragonflies, roaches, cicadas) appear. Frogs develop. Early reptiles with dry, scaly skins appear. They can lay eggs on land. Great swamps form coal deposits around the world, including along the margin of the continent of Gondwana. Gondwana moves westward to collide with our new continent during the Alleghenian Orogeny, forming the Avalon Terrane of southeastern New England. The collision completes the Appalachian Mountains which extend over much of Connecticut and the central part of the new super-continent of Pangaea.

270 million years (Permian)

Very high O_2 levels (up to 40 percent, compared with 21 percent today) allow huge insects to fly despite primitive respiratory systems. Reptiles (including the ancestors of modern mammals) become diverse and large. CO_2 has dropped again, and an ice age occurs across polar regions. The greatest mass extinction in history wipes out 90 percent of living species at the end of the Permian 250 million years ago. The extinction may have been caused by vast lava flows and volcanic gases or a bolide impact. The Appalachian Mountains still reach high, but are rapidly eroding.

225 million years (Triassic)

Life takes tens of millions of years to recover from the Permian-Triassic extinction. Reptiles grow large and diverse to crawl over land, swim the oceans and glide through the skies. Large forests of conifers, cycads, gingkos, and tree ferns mark a warm, but dry global climate. Mass extinction marks the end of the Triassic, again possibly due to meteor impacts or a series of volcanic events which flooded central Connecticut. This eliminates the large land reptiles and clears the way for dinosaurs to expand.

150 million years (Jurassic)

Huge plant-eating dinosaurs called sauropods walk on land. Large marine reptiles dominate the oceans. The first true birds evolve from theropod dinosaurs. Animals and plants become more diverse. The Atlantic Ocean has opened with a shoreline east of Connecticut, while once tall peaks erode rapidly.

120 million years (Cretaceous)

Flowering plants evolve and become as abundant as trees, grasses, herbs, shrubs, etc. Bees and butterflies follow. More birds and mammals evolve. Sea levels rise until southern Connecticut is beneath the shallow western Atlantic Ocean. The last of the "big five" mass extinctions marks an end to the age of dinosaurs, as well as all flying reptiles and the remaining marine reptiles, and the Cretaceous. This time, both a large volcanic lava event in India and a huge meteor impact may be responsible. The largest crater known on earth, buried in the western Yucatan Peninsula and Gulf of Mexico, provides compelling evidence of an asteroid impact.

50 million years (Tertiary)

Mammals and birds inherit the earth and, without competition from dinosaurs and pterosaurs, rapidly expand. Early primates evolve, and other mammals return to the sea as whales. The climate cools, although it still feels sub-tropical in Connecticut. The land slowly rises and the Cretaceous beach sands are washed away from southern Connecticut.

1 million years (Quaternary)

The Ice Age covers northern continental areas as well as Antarctica with sheets of continental ice up to a mile thick. Early humans flourish, learn to use tools and fire, and gradually come to dominate all other living things. The movements of thick ice sheets over Connecticut erode our mountains and valleys and later fill many of the valleys with thick sand and gravel deposits.

12,000 years (Recent)

The great sheets of ice melt back into Canada and most of the large Ice Age mammals of Connecticut die out. The first Native Americans move into Connecticut. The climate rapidly warms to its present state, and plants and animals familiar to us today inhabit our landscape.

Fossils 6

Eubrontes footprint near Mount Tom, Holyoke, Massachusetts

Humans have been fascinated by fossils from the time early hominids first sought shelter in caves—and perhaps earlier. Even before people came to appreciate fossils' subtle meanings they were charmed by their variety and mimicry. At once they were as cold as stone and all but alive.

Fossils reveal even more sides today. They can be formed by any of several different natural processes and preserve details of living things as small as organic compounds and as large as dinosaurs. They can thrill by preserving incredible, finely-detailed records or tantalize by leaving out essential clues. Somehow, they are always intriguing.

The Connecticut Valley fossil record

It's said the only sure thing in life is death, but when it comes to fossilization, not even death is a sure thing. Most of the time, plants and animals decompose quickly after dying. The remains of some, however, become fossilized for a variety of reasons and can survive for hundreds of millions of years. Still others leave living traces in life that later fossilize and remain long after whatever made them disappeared.

Examples of many different processes of fossilization are found in the Connecticut Valley. Footprints and trace fossils are by far the most abundant. Many were preserved in the sediments that rapidly filled the valley by a process known as cementation. Fish were also commonly preserved among the sediments on lake bottoms. In rare cases, trees and animals were preserved as natural casts by a process of dissolution and replacement. In a handful of cases, reptile and dinosaur bones survived within sedimentary rock.

Cementation

For footprints and trace fossils to be preserved, they first had to be buried. The local geology and climate created conditions that were ideal for taking and covering many natural impressions.

Because the Connecticut Valley was a rift valley, it collected sediments washed or blown down out of the surrounding highlands at astonishing rates. "Continental rift valleys were very sensitive to climatic changes," says Paul Olsen, "and the accumulation rates were very, very high. For example, in the Portland Formation, which is one of the largest parts of the Connecticut Valley sequence, the accumulation rate was 20 meters [65 feet] every 20,000 years."

The high rate of sedimentation worked to level and flatten the valley floor and made it easy for water to collect—forming streams, ponds and lakes. Water levels rose and fell following climatic cycles. Rainy seasons filled the lakes and flooded surrounding shorelines and mudflats. Dry seasons left lakes to evaporate and baked mudflats hard and dry.

Muddy shorelines that were covered with dinosaur footprints one week might be flooded the next. If the mud were of the right consistency, and lake levels rose slowly enough, footprints might

The footprint Otozoum, from the Moody Footprint Quarry

remain until they were covered by organic material, minerals and particles of clay that clouded the lake water and settled on the bottom in layers of silt.

Once covered, impressions were protected within the sediments. The sediments could later be lithified (turned to stone) by minerals such as calcium carbonate, iron oxide or silicon dioxide dissolved in groundwater. Over time, the minerals reacted to cement grains of sand and mud together, turning footprints into geologic features that last for immensely long periods of time. "If you go out to your average meter of Portland Formation," says Paul, "you'll find footprints."

The process of cementation worked to preserve traces of the past, from footprints to impressions made by weather. Edward Hitchcock described impressions he found in sandstone that appeared to record a brief interval of a passing rain shower: "The same surface over which the animals of sandstone days walked, often shows numerous minute hemispherical impressions most clearly refferible [sic] to rain, for rain now produces exactly the same markings upon mud. If the surface thus impressed were sun dried, so that when water brought in a layer of mud over the spot, it did not wash away the impressions, and the whole was ultimately converted into stone, on splitting these layers apart, on the lower one we should find depressions, and on the under side of the upper one, protuberances or casts of rain drops. Such we do find: the phenomena being parallel to these of the tracks."

Preservation in lakes

The large lakes of the Connecticut Valley played a central role in preserving much of what is known of local life in the Mesozoic, including fossil fish. It was the nature of the shorelines that preserved animal footprints and the chemistry of the water that led to the preservation of fish.

Anyone who has ever dived into a lake in early spring is familiar with a common quality of lake water: it is often separated in layers. It may be warm near the surface, but let your legs drop down and you will feel how water in the layer just below can be much cooler. Layers of lake water can differ in other ways as well. Nutrients that fish and other aquatic life rely on may become less concentrated in deeper layers. The deeper the water gets, the less sunlight filters down and the less oxygen is dissolved in the water.

All these things make lake bottoms relatively uninhabitable, but ideal for preserving fossils. Dead fish that sink to the bottom may remain there until they are buried by silt filtering down from above. Eventually, the fish become fossilized in layers of silt and mud at the lake bottom that lithify to form rocks known as shales.

Dissolution & replacement

In some cases, it is even possible for sedimentary stone to make a cast of a plant or animal after it has decomposed. The action of the ground water can fill a space where soft tissue had been with other minerals. They become molded in the shape left by the organism and later harden into a cast.

One of the first people in the Connecticut Valley to recognize fossils preserved by dissolution and replacement was the Middletown physician and amateur fossil hunter, Dr. Joseph Barrett. Barrett found natural casts of plants and trees in local brownstone quarries. The process came to be known after Barrett shared his experiences with scientists, including Edward Hitchcock.

Since that time, several local reptiles have come to be known from natural casts, including specimens of *Stegomus* and *Stegomosuchus* and the partial skeleton of a small theropod dinosaur. The animals' bones were worn away, but their shapes were preserved in natural casts by a process similar to the way footprints were preserved.

Sedimentation

It's most often the hard parts of animals that are preserved by fossilization. Bones have a better chance of surviving long enough to be preserved. Only under rare circumstances is soft tissue preserved. Mammoths with skin and hair have been freeze-dried in arctic permafrost. People have been found in bogs with skin turned to leather. There are specimens of dinosaurs with what appear to be pieces of skin, some even with feathers, but these are exceptions.

More typically, soft tissues decompose after an animal dies. In some cases, bones may survive to be buried by accumulating sediments and remain embedded in sedimentary rock, or matrix, for hundreds of millions of years.

Interpreting fossil footprints

Footprints are the most abundant forms of fossil evidence in the Connecticut Valley. With them the challenge has always been the same. How do you discover extinct animals with little more than footprints to go on? Hitchcock realized this problem when he first began to describe the footprints that are most abundant in the valley. Unless a fossil hunter is fortunate enough to find a well-preserved dinosaur dead in its tracks at the end of a series of fossil footprints, there is no way to be sure which animal made those footprints.

In his first study in 1836, Hitchcock proposed a simple, straightforward solution. Rather than attempt to connect or correlate the footprint makers with animals known from fossil bones or other evidence, Hitchcock concentrated on classifying the footprints. He gave names to the footmarks and not to the animals. "I include all the varieties of tracks under the name Ornithichnites; signifying stony bird-tracks," he explained in the report, "and if it be convenient to speak of the subject as a distinct branch of knowledge, I should call it Ornithichnology."

Hitchcock's approach was to name footprints based on his observations. "It should be here noted that Hitchcock clearly describes the species," Lull wrote, "but that the higher names are based on ideas, not on any specific specimen, i.e. on 'bird tracks,' either 'thick toed' or 'slender toed.'"

Hitchcock shortened the term ornithichnology to expand its meaning a year later. "I arrange all the footmarks under the general term Ichnites," he wrote. The study of fossil footmarks came to be known as ichnology. It included studies he made of different types of footprints beyond just the marks he believed were made by birds. Footprints classified in groups have since come to be referred to as ichnotaxa; individual types of footprints are known as ichnospecies.

Many of the names Hitchcock originally gave to footprints have since been changed multiple times. Some were misidentified and there is a lot of confusion over how footprints were named and renamed, classified and reclassified. However, the system Hitchcock devised and the ichnotaxa he described remain widely used standards of comparison.

Filling in the tracks

Hitchcock began to name tracks based on what he'd learned

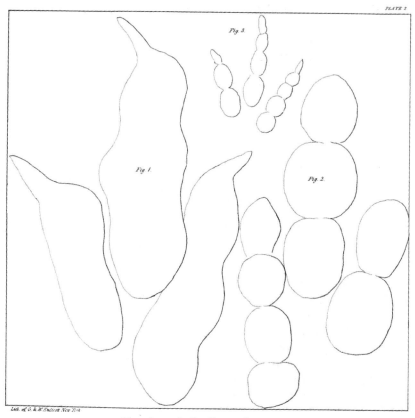

*Sketches of Grallator footprints
from the report Hitchcock published in 1848.*

of the trackmakers in 1845. By then most geologists had come
to accept the footprints as real fossils, and Hitchcock had
developed an acute sense for trackmakers from poring over slabs of
brownstone.

"I ought to say," he wrote, "that for several years, I merely
gave names to these tracks with reference to their supposed
affinities, such as Ornithichnites, or stony bird-tracks;
Sauroidichnites, or like the tracks of Saurians, &c. But more
recently, I have named the animals that made the tracks; as

Brontozoum giganteum, or the huge animal giant; *Polemarchus gigas,* the huge leader in war; *Ancryropus heteroclitus,* or the strange anchor-footed animal, &c., &c."

Hitchcock came up with more than thirty ways to measure footprints and came to understand many in great detail. He made notes of whether a trackmaker showed signs of walking on two or four feet and the size and shape of the feet. He counted toes, looked for claw marks or evidence of webbed feet, measured the length of an animal's stride and more.

"Those thirty characteristics, based upon the principles of comparative anatomy and zoology, will afford us, it seems to me, reliable grounds from which to judge of an animal from its track. Some of the characters are, of course, far less decisive than others, and few of them would singly remove all doubt; but, if several of them conspire, they constitute strong evidence . . . I think we might decide with a good degree of confidence upon the following:

1. Whether the animal is vertebral or invertebral
2. Whether a biped, quadruped, or multiped.
3. To which of the four great classes of vertebrates, or the nine classes of invertebrates, it belongs.
4. To what order. This is more difficult, and we should often fail.
5. To what genus. This is sometimes more difficult; for the feet of many genera are too much alike to be distinguished by their tracks. This difficulty, however, would tend to the formation of too few rather than too many genera.
6. To what species. And since a specific description embraces the whole animal, perhaps we should reach the truth more often as to species than to genera or classes."

In making his measures, Hitchcock had been greatly influenced by the approach French anatomist Georges Cuvier took to discovering animals from fossil bones and his principle of the correlation of parts. Hitchcock made his own argument for the

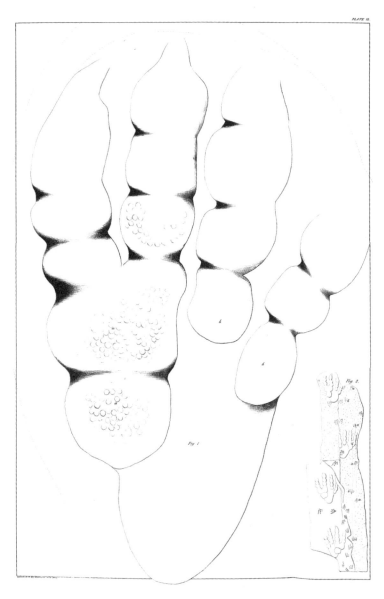

Sketches of the Otozoum footprint and of a series of footprints, or trackway, from the report Hitchcock published in 1848.

utility of footprint evidence: "The grounds on which I propose to name and describe the animals that made the fossil footmarks, are derived from comparative anatomy and zoology. These sciences show a mathematically exact relation to exist, not only between different classes and families of animals, but between different parts of animals… It is like an equation in algebra; having the known quantities on one side, we can ascertain the unknown upon the other side. The result may sometimes be ambiguous, as it is in quadratic equations; but the relations between the different parts in animals is probably as certain as between quantities in mathematics."

HITCHCOCK'S TALLY

It was an admirable objective, but in practice, reconstructing dinosaurs from footprints has proved far more difficult and is perhaps impossible. Comparative anatomy depends on having other animals of a similar type with which comparisons can be made, and few Mesozoic animals were available to Hitchcock. Only a handful of dinosaurs had by then been described and Hitchcock, for the most part, believed he was looking at the footmarks of birds.

As a result, he classified his discoveries in a number of groups, some of which later proved inaccurate. Others became outdated, which he anticipated: "I expect that future discoveries will strike out some of these species: but my prediction is, that they will bring a still larger number of new ones to light."

Number of localities of Tracks in the Valley thus far discovered,	38
Length of the sandstone belt containing the tracks,	90 miles
Width of the sandstone belt containing the tracks,	2 or 3 miles
Whole number of species in the Valley described above,	119
Number of Bipeds,	31
Number of Quadrapeds,	55
With more than four feet,	18

Without proper feet,	12
With an uncertain number,	3
Marsupialoid Animals,	5
Thick-toed birds,	14
Narrow-toed birds,	17
Ornithoid Lizards or Batrachians,	10
Lizards,	17
Batrachians, the frog and salamander family,	11
Chelonians, the Tortoise family,	8
Fishes,	4
Crustaceans, Myriapods and Insects,	18
Annelids, the naked worms,	8
Of uncertain place,	6

One notable difference between Hitchcock's classification and current views of the evidence is his classification of the ichnogenera *Anomoepus* as a "marsupialoid." Having little with which to compare its tracks, Hitchcock suspected it might have been an early animal, one with feet in some ways similar to those of a dog: "At the head of the list stand five species, which I have denominated Marsupialoid, that is animals appearing like Marsupials. These, it is well known, belong to the order Mammalia of zoologists; and although the lowest in organization of that family, yet they are regarded as higher than birds and reptiles . . . It is with much hesitation that I refer five species from their tracks, not to marsupials proper, but to Marsupialoids. Yet I am sometimes inclined to believe that a large part of the fifty-four quadrupeds which I have described, belong to this family; for very many of them have unequal feet, and this is a common character among living marsupials."

The footprint Hitchcock refers to is recognized today as that of an ornithischian dinosaur and not a mammal or a marsupial. Without an adequate standard of comparison, Hitchcock was left to guess at the nature of the trackmaker and to reflect what are now antiquated views of mammals and marsupials.

A current view of the footprints

Paleontologists have since refined some knowledge about the footprints, but a good deal of confusion and outdated information remains. Besides the problems that occurred with Hitchcock's efforts to describe the trackmakers, others' efforts to update his work in some cases did more harm than good.

Hitchcock went back and changed many descriptions and names several times. Following his death, Hitchcock's son, Charles, made more changes to his father's work. Dr. O. P. Hay made an attempt at revising the names in 1902. Richard Swann Lull made many more revisions beginning in 1904. The result was that tracks were classified many times in many ways, and, in all likelihood, into more groups than there were animals to account for them.

The challenge of classifying the footprints still remains. It has been taken up by Paul Olsen and his colleague, Emma Rainforth, a leading authority on footprints. These two have worked for years at straightening out what they can.

Paul and Emma argue that there were likely far fewer footprint makers, especially among the dinosaurs, than Edward Hitchcock, Charles Hitchcock or Richard Swann Lull concluded there were. They point out that many differences in size or other aspects of the footprints likely reflect natural variations between individuals of different ages or of different sexes.

"Because footprints are the result of an animal interacting with a substrate [like a muddy lakeshore] interpretation of footprints is more subtle and difficult than body fossils," says Paul. "The form of footprints is profoundly influenced by the behavior of the animal and the behavior of what the animal walks on. In addition, different species of animals often have nearly identical feet, and juveniles often have feet of different proportions than adults."

As is often the case in science, certain aspects of the early work and Lull's revisions don't hold up to today's scrutiny. "That's not to denigrate the work," Paul explains. "They were extremely

Otozoum footprints at the Portland Public Library, Connecticut

important works and still are. It's amazing that Lull's 1953 book is still available—and people still use it a lot."

The fact is that a lot has changed in paleontology since the 1950s. Trying to reconcile new conceptions with old ideas can be a daunting task. "When we try to bring things up to modern standards it's very, very difficult," Paul says. "You have to actually look at the specimens and go through them very carefully. I'll show you the problem," he says, reaching for a report he'd recently published. "This is one specific kind of footprint, called *Anomoepus*, that was described by Lull. To clean it up required a substantial paper, and it's just one name. There are 47 such names in Lull and I can't write a paper like this for each one."

Another example lies with the footprint known as *Anchisauripus*. "*Anchisauripus* is a misnomer," Paul argues. "It means 'foot of *Anchisaurus*.' That was Lull making a new genus out of something he shouldn't have. He named it after *Anchisaurus* because those were the bones that had been found, but there's no similarity [between the footprint known as *Anomoepus* and the actual foot structure of *Anchisaurus*]. You have to remember that all dinosaurs, like *Coelophysis*, weren't known at the time Lull began his work. So, they didn't know as much about foot structure."

Bones versus footprints

The uncertainty surrounding footprint evidence led to it sometimes being considered less favorably in comparison to bone evidence. More recently, footprint specialists like Paul and Emma and Martin Lockley have done a great deal to change old biases against footprints and to show how they are useful in ways bones are not.

There are many ways to describe the differences between fossil footprints and fossil bones. Footprints are evidence of living dinosaurs; bones are evidence of dead dinosaurs. Footprints are found in situ, alongside traces of the environment in which dinosaurs lived; it can be difficult to learn much about the environment from bones. Footprints reveal aspects of dinosaur behavior that bones cannot. And, of course, bones have historically been pursued as plunder; footprints hold a different sort of fascination altogether.

The simple truth is that there are limits to both. Each has its strengths and weaknesses. There are some things that can be learned from bones that cannot be learned from footprints, just as footprints reveal things bones cannot. Still, tracks seem to have been given short shrift.

"Tracks had been neglected," notes Martin Lockley. "Skeptics said, 'well, they're not real evidence. You have to have the hard, solid evidence bones give you.' And I say, oh, so tracks are not evidence? They're not real? Well—tracks are real!

"In the last twenty years dinosaur track sites have been discovered and documented all around the world," Martin continues. "Coming out of that, we've seen some significant new interpretations of the behavior and distribution of dinosaurs in space and time. Ultimately, bones and tracks will have to be considered together. Today, we compare bones and tracks like they're separate fields, but they go together. Bones and tracks are completely integrated pieces of the same jigsaw puzzle."

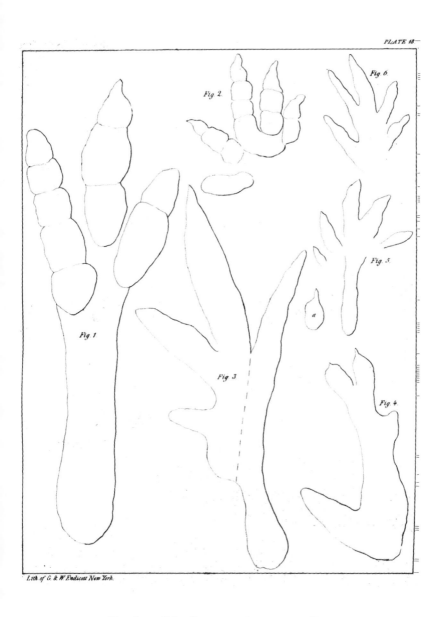

PLATE 48

*Sketches of the footprint Anomoepus from
the report Hitchcock published in 1848*

103

Pieces of the same puzzle

"Dinosaur tracks are evidence of living animals rather than dead," says Martin. "Very often bones tell us more about how the animal died and was preserved, which is useful, but tracks tell us where the animal was going, exactly the habitat it was living in and so forth."

As Martin observes, bone evidence is best for the marvelous detail it offers about individual animals. Most dinosaurs are known today from the shapes of their bones and the way they fit together. A meat-eating theropod can be distinguished from a plant-eating prosauropod from just a few bones—even fragments of bones. In many cases, differences between even very closely related dinosaurs can be recognized.

On the other hand, bones may not reveal as much about when or where a dinosaur known only from bones actually lived. All it takes is a flash flood and bones can end up among rocks formed in a different age or in a different environment from the one in which a dinosaur belonged. "With bones there is always this uncertainty," Martin says. "Did the animal really live in this habitat or were the bones washed in?"

Footprint evidence has proved very useful for determining when different types of animals lived and died. There is little question that they are the same age as the rocks that contain them and that they are associated with the environment that existed when the rocks were formed. Footprints can be linked with fossil pollen and other evidence to reveal quite a bit about habitat and other plants and animals in the community at the time.

A Eubrontes footprint at the Mount Tom reservation, Holyoke, Massachusetts

Footprints can also reveal

a great deal about behavior. "As far as individual behavior [goes]," Martin observes, "there have been efforts to calculate dinosaur speed and show that by and large there were a significant number of theropods capable of moving pretty fast. We've had other discoveries, such as evidence of limping dinosaurs taking alternate short and long steps.

A cast of the bones of Podokesaurus discovered in South Hadley, Massachusetts.
Courtesy of the Peabody Museum of Natural History, Yale University, New Haven, CT

"As far as social behavior [goes]," Martin continues, "one of the big discoveries that has attracted attention is evidence that most of the herbivorous dinosaurs were gregarious. There seems to be evidence from parallel trackways, especially among ornithopod dinosaurs and sauropod dinosaurs, that they frequently traveled in large groups."

Some tracks even suggest dinosaurs may have evolved complex herding behaviors. Edward Hitchcock was the first to raise this possibility in the 1830s based on observations he made about a trackway near Mount Tom, in Holyoke, Massachusetts. John Ostrom wrote about studies he made of this site in 1972 and discussed the Mount Tom footprints along with evidence from several other sites.

Martin has discussed other examples at sites he has studied. "In the West, we have three sites from the Late Jurassic and Cretaceous where there's an organic flow to the tracks," Martin observes. "The animals were moving like a single organism, in a synchronized 'entrainment' or rhythm. These animals would all veer to the right, then they would all veer to the left and then they would all veer to the right again."

Martin thinks we will learn more about populations of dinosaurs and their interactions in the future. "There's enough data [from these] sites to begin to investigate the structure of populations. Do we have populations where there is a whole range of sizes from young, relatively young dinosaurs to fully-grown ones, or are they clustered? Or do you get groups of two sizes or one size?"

Martin knows there will always be some paleontologists who remain skeptical of footprint evidence. "They're going to say it's not very reliable evidence or how do you know if you're dealing with differences between juveniles and adults or males and females." He believes, however, that his own work now stands up to the true test of science: predictability. "Predictability is always considered important in science. I would say that if someone finds a new site, in a formation I am familiar with, I could predict what tracks are going to be found there in more than nine cases out of ten.

"This convinces me that the tracks are a reliable census of the animals that lived in a particular environment, represented by its formations. If they weren't, each new discovery would be unpredictable or random. That's not the case."

A biologist looks at fossil tracks

It's two o'clock in the morning—and still light out. Stephen Gatesy sits on a hillside overlooking Greenland's Fleming Fjord, fingers covered in Krazy Glue, piecing together dinosaur tracks and staring out at the ice floes. This is not where he expected to be, but here he is, shivering on a slab of fossilized mud that an early theropod dinosaur, not even as tall as his own, six-foot plus frame, walked across 200 million years earlier.

Steve Gatesy in Greenland.
Courtesy, Steve Gatesy

Steve had been snug inside a university lab a few months before, studying the ways animals move their limbs to get from one place to another. In comparing the way birds move to the way crocodiles move, he hoped to learn not just the mechanics of their locomotion, but how various modes of locomotion evolved over time. At this point, Steve never thought fossil footprints could be of much use to him in his work. "I always felt that what we were seeing in tracks was just kind of where dinosaurs placed their feet, not how they placed their feet," Steve explains. "Take a dance chart as an example. They show left foot here, right foot there—but there is a lot more to dancing than putting your feet in the right place at the right time . . . If all we were seeing was where this thing put its foot, we were missing all the fun stuff. Anything that happens above ground level, between the sole of the foot and hip level, is essentially invisible."

Steve thought all the action was above ground. "A footprint wasn't going to tell you if an animal moved mostly at the knee or mostly at the hip. Did they move mostly at the ankle or mostly at the joint in the toes? Your typical footprint—nice pads, skin impressions, claws, the archetypal print—isn't going to tell you."

Steve's career took an unexpected turn in 1989 after a few of the more oddly shaped footprints in the sediments of the Fleming Fjord caught his eye. What he saw in the Greenland tracks was something no one had noticed in two centuries of studying footprints. The oddities Steve found were more than just simple impressions of a foot pressed flat on the ground like a rubber stamp on a sheet of paper. There was another kind of record altogether—more like the last, few frames in a movie of a living dinosaur walking.

The discovery led him in an entirely different direction from the one in which his career had been heading. As a biologist and anatomist, Steve was used to tossing pigeons down hallways to study how they moved their tails, or taking x-rays of crocodiles to record the ways they moved their legs. "I wasn't prepared to study dinosaur tracks," he says. "But I like to look at things from different angles."

If he was lucky, he realized, the Greenland tracks might not only provide a different way to look at how living reptiles and birds walk but also shed light on how locomotion evolved. They might even reveal clues as to how dinosaurs themselves had once walked.

Steve's colleagues couldn't imagine what he saw in fossilized mud. Steve was supposed to have a bright future in the land of the living. "How could you ever work on fossils?" they would ask him. "We don't completely understand how living animals walk." "You're right," he would reply, "but on the other side, there are paleontologists who never look at living animals—who just want to rub a few bones together and say, 'walk this way' without getting into the complexity of living animals."

Serendipity

Steve's is a classic story of looking for one thing only to find something else. "I went to Greenland in search of Late Triassic mammals," he says. "That's where we stumbled on these dinosaur tracks—thousands and thousands of dinosaur tracks." Nearly all had the distinctive, three-toed mark of theropod dinosaurs, and many were a lot like the early meat-eaters that left tracks in the Connecticut Valley.

"They were everywhere," he says. "We passed thousands of tracks a day—which was cool for the first few days—and then we started getting picky. We began to look for strange stuff. That was when we started running into these long, elongated tracks. We started getting these wacky things. The impressions were like slits around a bit of mud raised up in a big mound. The big mystery was, what was going on with them?"

The weird tracks were relatively few among thousands of distinct theropod tracks, but their appearance presented a real puzzle. Not only were the toes longer and thinner, it looked like

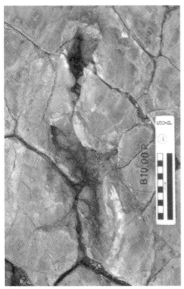
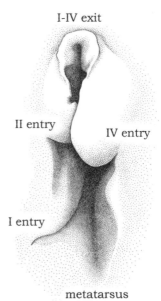

A Greenland theropod footprint (left) and a sketch showing the marks attributed to each of the animal's toes (right).
Courtesy, Steve Gatesy

there were the marks of four toes impressed in the mud—or one toe too many for them to be theropod footprints. The tracks just didn't add up.

Theropods walked on three toes, but they had two more rudimentary toes, to the rear of the foot and higher on the ankle. Technically, the larger of these, the hallux, counts as the first toe. The hallux is the same as a person's big toe and the one most birds use for gripping a perch. In the vernacular of anatomy and ichnology, the toes that theropods walked on and that are seen in their footprints, were the second, third and fourth toes (the same as a person's three middle toes). In theropods, the hallux was the only other toe substantial enough to possibly account for the impression of a fourth toe, but was ordinarily well off the ground when the animal walked.

Steve was stumped. He began spending long, Arctic nights

hunched over in his tent making crude sketches on graph paper. He and his colleagues simulated dinosaur toes walking through mud using their fingers. They made use of whatever they could to imagine what made the odd impressions at the Fleming Fjord.

Walking through the muddy slop of the summer thaw, an idea struck him. "Maybe these were the same animals that made all the tracks, but some got into this really, mucky-muck stuff which is all over Greenland when the melt comes," Steve says. "We were always ankle deep in mud, trying to find our way through." If the muck had people sinking ankle deep and affected the way they walked, maybe it also affected the way dinosaurs had walked.

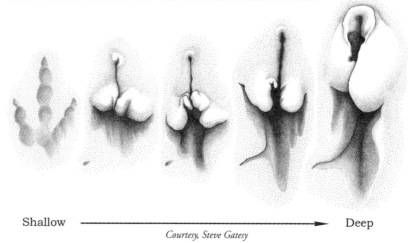

Shallow ⟶ Deep

Courtesy, Steve Gatesy

The light bulb

Back in his lab, Steve put the idea to the test. With graduate student Kevin Middleton, he designed an experiment to see how a turkey—a bird with a three-toed foot design similar to that of a theropod—made its way over a soft, mucky surface.

They imagined that the bird might make a sort of "snowshoe" movement the instant it felt itself sinking in sloppy ground, but that wasn't what the bird did—at all. Instead, the turkey stepped into the mud with its three toes spread wide—but rolled its foot up into a ball on the way out. "What we found, and this was the big shocker, was that the whole foot came out as a unit." Even more interesting was that it left behind an impression just like the odd-shaped footprints from Greenland.

"That was the light bulb going off," Steve says. The discovery encouraged him to go back to collect more fossils. When he put them together in a sequence things started to make sense. Steve saw that the Greenland tracks weren't flat-footed impressions of dinosaurs' feet, but records of movement their feet made when walking through the mud—a sort of Mesozoic mpeg stored on a fossilized hard disk.

"The traditional approach didn't work," Steve says. "Track people had fallen into the shorthand of saying, 'here's the second toe, here's the third toe, here's the fourth toe' … they talked about impressions as toes. That only works when a footprint is shallow and the toes make and leave the same impressions."

Interpreting footprints preserved in deep mud demanded a new approach. "What we found was a splash exactly where the second toe goes in and another that was created where all the toes

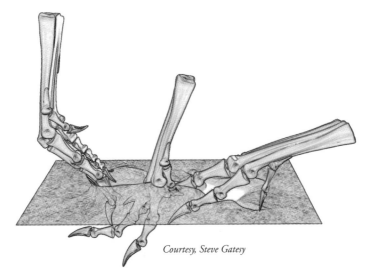

Courtesy, Steve Gatesy

come out. So, for that surface, we had one toe making two marks." Therefore, Steve concludes, "we can't just number the toes. We have to talk about events. That's what these fossils show. It's a sequence of positions, such that the foot is going in one place and out somewhere else, and the surface is only giving us part of the picture."

Go a little deeper and the true significance of deep prints becomes clear. They provide a record of how a theropod moved its foot during the time it took to step through the mud. What's left is an impression of the last places the foot contacted. "One of my students said, 'they are four-dimensional, with a time component built right in.' That made me look at tracks differently," Steve admits.

If it walks like a turkey

The result completely changed Steve's opinion of footprints. "For me, the guy who said I didn't think tracks can give the information I want, all of a sudden I've got what seems like a pretty unique source of information about foot movement and about the movement of the bottom part of the leg." Put together with what he'd already learned flying pigeons down halls, and x-raying crocodiles and running turkeys through mud, Steve thought he just might have something. "If you know what's going on with the foot you can say what's going on at the hip, the knee or the ankle—not with certainty, but better constrained than . . . previously."

It was time for Steve to go shopping for animation software, to borrow a foot from a skeleton of the small theropod known as *Coelophysis*, and to try and make dinosaurs walk again.

"Trying to figure out how you go back and reanimate fossils, that's the hard part," Steve says. "In the back of my mind I've got this set of legs. The legs keep walking—for 230 million years— while the body is changing. It's getting smaller. It's getting larger. It's changing proportionally. It's growing wings. It's doing all these things and yet, the animal is still walking."

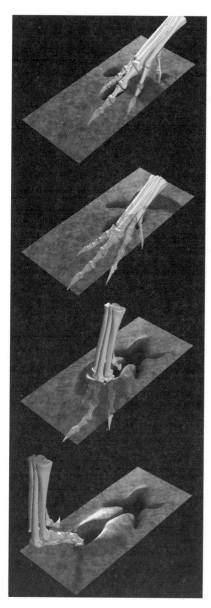

Courtesy, Steve Gatesy

Steve recreated the dinosaur's foot using a computer in his lab at Brown University. Once he had the bones programmed in, he began to play reanimator. "After a lot of work you end up with a foot that you can make dance Swan Lake," he laughs. The trick was to make it dance like a dinosaur. "We decided to start by using a turkey as a reference. Of all the infinite ways of making it move, let's give the foot the motion of a living theropod that we know is viable. And so, we made it walk like a turkey."

The computer kept track of where the foot was as it moved through an imaginary layer of mud. "We use a system that keeps track of where the foot has been," Steve says, "which is pretty non-intuitive for this thing that has all these little pieces moving in a very complicated way." Sure enough, the foot drew a shape along the surface just like the shapes found in Greenland. "It's still hypothesis," says Steve. "People take the computer work as either the truth or Jurassic Park, so

113

we're straddling the line."

Maybe so, but it seems to make sense. "I'm quite happy to have it be obvious or common sense. I think the concept is right and I think that's the appeal of the animation. I can draw it for you a thousand times, but watch the ten-second clip and you know immediately what I was trying to say."

Did dinosaurs walk like birds?

Steve isn't sure what his studies of birds and crocs and footprints imply about the theory that birds evolved from theropod dinosaurs. "Are they [the Greenland trackmakers] identical to birds? No. Are they similar to birds? They're similar in some ways, different in others. That's the level of understanding I think we can get to now," he explains. "The idea is that there is a composite of things going on. I guess the surprise for me is that the animals are doing things I didn't expect them to do."

Mistaken identity?

Word of Steve's discovery came as a surprise to Paul Olsen. Steve used footprints from Greenland, but Paul saw right away what his discovery meant in terms of the Connecticut Valley record. "This really was a pleasant surprise," Paul remembers. "There are many footprints Hitchcock called *Leptodactylous*. They were his thin-toed tracks, and there are a lot of them with funny arrangements of toes, very strange looking; the shapes are remarkable.

"I used to think they were just poorly preserved footprints. We had a term for them, called 'under tracks.' The idea was that the dinosaur would walk along, and he'd step on one layer and that track would be impressed on the layer underneath in a more vague sense. But I always had a problem with that because the underlying footprints should all be more and more gently curved.

"And then, Steve's paper came out," Paul says, "a marvelous discovery. It immediately explained what these footprints meant in a brand-new way. The shape is not the shape of the foot; it's the shape of its movement. All of a sudden, things which had no informational context to me, except indicating the water was shallow, now meant something about living animals."

Steve is pleased to receive such reviews and happy that his work has helped solve a mystery that went unsolved for so long. "We don't want to read all tracks literally, as toe or foot anatomy," Steve says. "I think that Hitchcock, like everyone who followed him, read these tracks literally.

"There are footprints like [the Greenland footprints] at Amherst. There's one sitting in a hallway at Yale. It's at the front of this book," Steve points out, flipping to a photograph in the introduction of Richard Swann Lull's *Triassic Life of the Connecticut Valley*. The tracks, collected at Turner's Falls, Massachusetts, and catalogued in the Peabody collection as YPM 2030, were identified by Lull as *Steropoides diversus*. It now seems they might merit another look. "They're not as pretty as those we found in Greenland," Steve says, "but these are described as four-toed, flat-footed things with a reversed, opposable first toe. That's what you'd get if you read this literally. You'd say it's got four toes, a heel print, a sole print, and a first toe that's opposite the fourth toe, and that's what Hitchcock said."

Steve Sauter's modern traces

Steve Sauter's family makes fun of him whenever he takes his camera out. "Not again!" they plead and tease when they see him getting ready to take another picture of the ground and record another of his modern traces.

The man who spends his days giving tours of the Hitchcock Collection of fossil traces spends his time off looking for fresh ones. He takes photographs of footprints and traces that animals and plants make in environments today and shows them to visitors as a way of explaining how dinosaurs left their marks in the Connecticut Valley.

Hitchcock conducted similar exercises for his students and

for doubters. "We have… an almost exact counterpart of. . . fossil footmarks, and the manner in which they were formed," he wrote. "Here we have . . . under our immediate inspection, the tracks of some thirteen species of animals . . . Here every rain storm or shower would leave pools of water, around and through which, various animals walked in search of food. Afterwards the water was dried up, and the clay so hardened that it could be split up. . . I know not how any one can escape the conclusion that the fossil footmarks . . . were formed in a similar manner. Indeed, I have always found these tracks . . . to be the most effectual argument I could use to convince those who were skeptical . . . and if they withstood this, I have regarded them as hopelessly unbelieving."

Steve's collection of modern traces includes many that bear an uncanny resemblance to those of the ancient past. They are a simple way to show the authenticity of ancient tracks, making them more fascinating and compelling.

Crow tracks

Leaf drag

Goose tracks

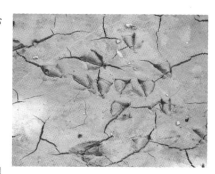

Ripples

Worm traces

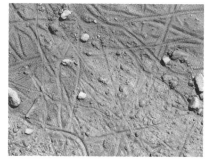

Many tracks

Extinction & Evolution 7

The skull of Hypsognathus fenneri, a primitive reptile known from the Triassic Period, including one specimen found in Meriden, Connecticut
Copyright©1995 Armand Morgan. Reprinted by permission.

I f there is one thing life teaches, it's that nothing lasts forever. Humans may see change as bringing things to an end. Yet the history of life over the past half a billion years tells another story. Change may instead be about new beginnings.

From the time primitive living cells first appear in the fossil record some 3.5 billion years ago, life has continually experimented with new and different ways to survive. Some flourished. They survived for long periods of time and led to many new forms. Others were dead ends.

Studies of fossils reveal many times in the past when living things grew and changed rapidly. These periods of growth and change are often marked by the first appearances of many new and sometimes bizarre forms of life.

The first of life's great expansions, known as the Cambrian Explosion, occurred in the oceans some 540 million years ago. It's known from fossils found at sites like the Burgess Shale in British Columbia, Canada. These fossils reveal a time when marine life grew quickly in number and in kind, and living things on earth became more different or more diverse.

Fossils also reveal times when life took big steps backward. These were times when the numbers and kinds of living things actually declined. Many of life's experiments reached their end, died and went extinct. Their extinctions are deduced from their last appearance in the fossil record, after which they are never found again. Mass extinctions occur when many forms of life from a variety of environments disappear in a relatively short period of time.

The greatest mass extinction of all time occurred some 250 million years ago, at the end of the Permian Period. Studies indicate that greater than 90 percent of life in the oceans and on land disappeared during the end-Permian extinction.

Paleontologists aren't sure what causes extinctions or if there are patterns or cycles to the way they occur. It is widely believed, however, that mass extinctions have occurred many times in the past—and have changed the course of life several times along the way.

Extinctions and the expansion of the dinosaurs

In the Triassic Period, following the Permian, the world slowly recovered. It gradually grew robust again and came to be filled with many new and different forms of life. On land, reptiles grew to be the dominant form of life.

Not until tens of millions of years after this recovery did dinosaurs evolve. The first appeared in the Late Triassic, between 230 and 225 million years ago. At first, they numbered only a few and were surprisingly small. These dinosaurs had to compete with more numerous, diverse and often larger reptiles for their survival.

By 200 million years ago, the balance of power on land had shifted. According to the fossil record, many primitive reptiles went extinct. The ecological niches they occupied—plant-eater spaces and meat-eater spaces—became available. Nature, it's said, abhors a vacuum, and the theory is that the animals best suited to move into these empty spaces were dinosaurs.

There are different opinions as to exactly when dinosaurs expanded and came to dominate life on earth, but their initial success traces to sometime in Late Triassic or Early Jurassic. In a sort of prehistoric game of musical chairs, when the music stopped primitive reptiles were left standing and dinosaurs took the empty seats.

Paul Olsen believes dinosaurs first grew large and diverse after the extinction at the Triassic-Jurassic boundary 201 million years ago. He imagines it was a relatively sudden event, one deadly enough to bring down a world filled by more primitive reptiles and usher in the age of dinosaurs.

What is unique about the Connecticut Valley and the rift valleys of the East Coast is the record they kept of the world at the time of the Triassic-Jurassic boundary. Paul argues that these valleys provide the most reliable evidence of how dinosaurs came to flourish that is available anywhere on the globe. His vision of a Triassic-Jurassic mass extinction, and the effects it had on life, frames much of what is now known about the Connecticut Valley during the Mesozoic Era.

Early in the age of dinosaurs

The Connecticut Valley fossil record remains vital because of the picture it provides of the world early in the age of dinosaurs. The record dates from the earliest Jurassic, just over the Triassic-Jurassic boundary, to the time Paul believes marks the first great expansion of dinosaurs.

Dinosaurs from the Connecticut Valley lived long before the many better-known dinosaurs, such as *Apatosaurus*, *Triceratops*,

Stegosaurus and *Tyrannosaurus.* These familiar giants didn't appear until tens or hundreds of millions of years later, during the Late Jurassic and Cretaceous Periods. They represent dinosaurs at or near the peak of their success. Connecticut Valley fossils reveal dinosaurs as they were much earlier, near the beginning of their long history.

Many of the body types, adaptations and behaviors perfected in dinosaurs of the Late Jurassic and Cretaceous appeared first in early dinosaurs, including many known from the valley. The long necks, big bellies, and plant-eating behavior evident from the bones of the local prosauropods *Anchisaurus* and *Ammosaurus,* and the footprint *Otozoum,* led in directions similar to those the plant-eaters took much later, when they grew into behemoths like *Apatosaurus.*

There are also similarities between meat-eating, theropod dinosaurs once common in the valley, evidenced by the bones of *Podokesaurus* and the footprints known as *Grallator* and *Eubrontes,* and the legendary theropods that appeared much later, such as *Tyrannosaurus rex.*

These similarities make the valley especially interesting to paleontologists seeking to understand the secrets of the dinosaurs' success. The place to start is often at the beginning, and few places offer as good a record of the dinosaur's beginning as the Connecticut Valley.

The Triassic-Jurassic mass extinction

"In the Triassic," Paul explains, "you have a rather rapid-fire series of events. You have the evolution of new groups without much in the way of extinction of old groups. The world is exceptionally full of different life forms. There is no inkling that anything is going to change and then—all of a sudden—half of everything is gone."

Within a relatively short period of time, Paul says, the world went from a place that supported several different types of environments, populated by a variety of different plants and animals, to a place where a basic environment became typical around the globe and was populated by far fewer plants and animals. It was what he describes as a "day-after" sort of world, suddenly made much less diverse, its future resting on a few hardy survivors.

Any of a number or combination of things might have caused the catastrophe at the Triassic-Jurassic boundary. The extinction may have resulted from radical changes in climate. Paul suspects it was the result of an asteroid or comet striking the earth. Greg McHone thinks perhaps vast floods of lava spilling out over large areas of the earth at very near the same time might have left much of it uninhabitable. Whatever the cause, it had to be something capable of causing dramatic, global change in a short period of time.

The world in the Late Triassic

The world in the Late Triassic Period was what Paul and his colleagues have described as a "hot house" world. The atmosphere contained very high concentrations of carbon dioxide, the so-called "greenhouse gas" being generated in large amounts today, and the earth had warmed enough to melt the polar ice caps. The continents were pressed together in a huge super-continent, known as Pangaea. Near the center of this vast landmass was the region that would eventually become New England.

By the middle of the Triassic, the same geologic forces that had pieced Pangaea together a hundred million years earlier were working to pull it apart. What followed was a series of events geologists describe as rifting. The earth's crust was stretched so thin that it cracked and settled in places, opening many so-called "rift" valleys. By the Late Triassic, a series of rift valleys had formed along what would become eastern North America, including the Connecticut rift valley.

If you could have walked from north to south across Pangaea in the Late Triassic, you would have passed through several distinct types of natural environments that Paul describes as provinces. Each province sustained its own indigenous communities of plants and animals adapted to its conditions.

Plant life included many types of ferns, cycads, horsetails and conifers. Fish and freshwater clams were abundant in lakes and rivers. On land, tetrapods including reptiles and amphibians grew numerous and more diverse.

Over the course of time, tetrapods changed greatly. The Early Triassic was dominated by a group of tetrapods known as synapsids, recognized by characteristics of their skulls. Primitive synapsids include such animals as the "finback" *Dimetrodon* which went extinct at the end of the Permian. Synapsids grew more diverse and led to the appearance of the first mammals before their numbers gradually declined in the Late Triassic, only to rebound in the Tertiary.

Synapsids were replaced in many environments by the appearance of a new group of reptiles, the archosaurs, which included the first dinosaurs in the Late Triassic. "By the time you get into the Late Triassic," Paul says, "dinosaurs are becoming more abundant, but there are also very large numbers of nondinosaurian herbivores and carnivores, and it's not obvious which are dominant.

"There were no large, dinosaurian herbivores in the tropics at all," Paul continues. "There were some fairly large ones in the higher latitudes, but not in the tropics. There are nondinosaurian carnivores [such as *Postosuchus*] that are larger and

A rendering of the super-continent Pangaea by Paul E. Olsen
Courtesy, Paul E. Olsen

more abundant than the carnivorous dinosaurs. The largest of the carnivorous dinosaurs had hips not much higher than a man's head. They were not what we consider very large dinosaurs and there were very few kinds."

New England in the Late Triassic

New England's location near the middle of Pangaea determined its climate. Far inland and just north of the equator, it was a hot and dry place, similar perhaps to regions in East Africa or Mexico today. Seasonal changes were likely greater in this interior region, marked by hot summers and cool winters.

Among the tetrapods known to have existed locally in the latest Triassic were *Aetosaurus* (formerly referred to as *Stegomus*, a kind of small, armored, plant-eating reptile known as an aetosaur), *Hypsognathus* (another small, primitive reptile known as a procolophonid) and a lizardlike reptile similar to the living reptile *Sphenodon*. There were crocodylomorphs (distant cousins of modern crocodiles) such as *Erpetosuchus* which had legs long enough that it may have been able to run at a gallop. There were also primitive archosaurs such as phytosaurs, animals recognizable for their long, narrow, toothy snouts and big nostrils.

Some paleontologists suspect that large amphibians, such as *Metoposaurus*, also inhabited the valley. They are known from similar environments of the same age in eastern North America, but evidence of them has not been found in the Connecticut Valley. And there probably were dinosaurs, the early models, as they were not long after they first appeared. Paul's studies suggest that through the Late Triassic they gradually grew larger and more abundant.

At least two dinosaurs may have been present in the Connecticut Valley in the Late Triassic, but skeletal evidence of them has not been found. The footprints called *Atreipus* are known from the Newark rift basin of New Jersey and may have been made by a small, plant-eating, ornithischian dinosaur. Small theropod

A model of a phytosaur known from the Triassic Period, created by paleontologist Donald Baird for Richard Rush Studio, Chicago.

dinosaurs from the Early Jurassic, like those thought to have made the footprint *Grallator*, may have also been present in Connecticut in the Late Triassic. No evidence of these dinosaurs from that time was preserved.

At the boundary: A fireball from space?

Paul has concluded that the great diversity of life that existed in the world until the Late Triassic came to a sudden end 201 million years ago. Studies Paul and his colleagues have made of the sandstones of North American rift valleys, and the plant and animal fossils found within, indicate that was when life made an abrupt change in the course it had long charted. Fifty million years of evolution were irreversibly disrupted in perhaps 20,000 years or less. The question Paul has sought for decades to answer is why? He says the evidence points to a sudden event that was significant enough to affect natural communities around the globe. What he's found so far has proved tantalizing, if not conclusive.

Two possibilities emerge as potential culprits. The cause of the Triassic-Jurassic mass extinction, in Paul's mind, was likely an asteroid or comet that came flying through space to collide with the earth.

Asteroid impacts are suspected to have caused global disasters several times in the past. An impact somewhere in the southern hemisphere, perhaps in western Australia, may have caused the end-Permian extinction 251 million years ago. Another asteroid, which left a huge crater in the earth along Mexico's Yucatan Peninsula, is blamed for the extinction that ended the reign of terrestrial dinosaurs 65 million years ago.

The theory is that impacts caused by asteroids colliding with the earth have had devastating effects. These asteroids, or bolides, are thought to have exploded with incredible force, enough to set large areas around the impact craters ablaze and to spew large volumes of smoke, dust and debris into the atmosphere.

A short time after a collision, dark clouds of smoke would rise into the upper atmosphere and be carried swiftly around the globe. Smoke would blot out the sun and plunge the world into cold and darkness. The delicate balance of ecosystems would be disrupted, and many would cease to function. Lacking light for photosynthesis, plants would wither and freeze. Animals would be left to starve.

There have been dramatic examples in recent years of just how

The Triassic reptile, Aetosaurus, created by paleontologist Donald Baird for the Richard Rush Studio, Chicago.
Courtesy, Paul E. Olsen

quickly toxic clouds of gas and soot can spread when fueled by fire and heat. In 1980, the eruption of Mount St. Helens sent smoke and ash across several states and across the Pacific. An explosion and fire at the Chernobyl nuclear power plant in 1986 sent clouds of radioactive particles across thousands of miles, reaching Europe and parts of Asia and North America within a few weeks. The remnants of both events are still easily detected in the soil in many of the affected areas.

As much evidence as Paul has to support his theory, a key piece is still missing: an impact site. A site near Manicouagan, Quebec, Canada, promised at first to be just the sort of "smoking crater" he was looking for, but has yet to be shown to be the right age. Radiometric dating of the crater done after Paul wrote about it in 1987 suggested that the crater was formed as much as 12 million years too early. Further efforts to determine the age of the crater may put the crater's age closer to the boundary.

While Paul continues his search for evidence, he acknowledges that other geological events might also have caused the disaster. Some geologists now suspect that at nearly the same time as a comet or asteroid may have hit, vast floods of lava spilled out over large areas of the world, including New England. While lava is known to have flowed in the rift valleys of eastern North America around this time, evidence obtained so far suggests that intervals of volcanic activity (or volcanism) occurred after the Triassic-Jurassic boundary—or thousands of years too late to have caused the extinctions.

Geologist Greg McHone believes the true nature of these volcanic events remains to be discovered. He believes periods of volcanism may well have occurred at the Triassic-Jurassic boundary—and perhaps extended beyond the rift valleys. Greg is one of a group of geologists working to test the hypothesis that central Pangaea was once flooded by vast amounts of lava across a region they refer to as the Central Atlantic Magmatic Province

(CAMP). If widespread intervals of volcanism did occur they may have caused or contributed to a period of extinction at the end of the Triassic and the beginning of the Jurassic.

Boiling hot lava?

In the hills behind the library in Woodbury, Connecticut, are rocks few people besides Greg notice. Greg comes here, to the Pomperaug Valley, to look for them. He believes the ridges along the walk up to the fire tower, with its magnificent views, are the remains of flood lavas of the CAMP.

There is evidence that lava flowed over and through the earth's crust in the Connecticut Valley three times. Relatively short periods of volcanism were followed by longer intervals of dormancy and sedimentation. Paul Olsen has documented how volcanic activity in the valley extended over a period of just under 600,000 years.

Greg believes that evidence of volcanic dikes and sills (systems that fed molten rock, or magma, through the earth's crust) found up and down eastern North America indicate the CAMP extended much further. He argues that volcanic activity may have left a

The Krafla fissure eruptions of Iceland

129

large portion of Pangaea uninhabitable—and may have pushed living things to the brink of extinction. Greg argues that if CAMP lavas were not the sole cause of a Triassic-Jurassic mass extinction they must be considered a part of a chain of events that led to the catastrophe.

The evidence

Greg believes evidence of CAMP lavas can be found today in the traprock ridges that run north to south through the Connecticut Valley, behind the Woodbury Library in the smaller Pomperaug Valley of southwestern Connecticut, across New England and in areas encircling the Atlantic Ocean. These ridges reveal how the lavas long ago cooled and crystallized to form the geometric columns of beautiful gray rock known as basalt. The same forces of erosion that carried away high mountains that once existed along the East Coast and about the Connecticut Valley may also have carried away CAMP basalts, except for the traprock ridges.

There is additional evidence below ground. The three lava floods are easily recognizable today in the Connecticut Valley's layer cake of sediments. Working up from the lower levels, the earliest lava flow to appear is a layer known as the Talcott Basalt. Above it are the lake muds and sands and sediments of the Shuttle Meadow Formation. A second lava flow, the Holyoke Basalt, follows next with another layer of lake muds and sands known as the East Berlin Formation. The Hampden Basalt was the last flow. It is buried in places beneath the Portland Arkose, a layer of brownstone that preserved many dinosaur footprints.

Greg estimates that CAMP lavas and underground dikes and sills extended across an area of nearly three million square miles. "The province extended within Pangaea from Brazil northeastward across western Africa, Iberia, and northwestern France, and from Africa westward through eastern and southern North America," Greg says, "as far as Texas and the Gulf of Mexico."

Lava fountains that formed above fissure eruptions may have reached a mile high. In places, layers of volcanic rock known as basalts were deposited hundreds of feet deep. Greg estimates as much as 600,000 cubic miles of lava spread over the earth's surface or just beneath it in cracks between layers of bedrock.

Volcanism & extinctions

Events of the magnitude of CAMP lavas occurred several times in the past. Known as LIPs, or Large Igneous Provinces, they mark times when geologic processes deep within the earth, in the section known as the mantle, pushed liquid rock up in such a way as to cause dramatic repercussions at the surface. During the Mesozoic these processes were enough to contribute to the breakup of the super-continent. Over time, they may also have influenced the course of life.

One of the great mysteries surrounding LIPs is the fact that they coincide with several of the greatest mass extinctions ever known. Early flood lavas, known as the Siberian Traps, flowed at the time of the end-Permian extinction. Greg's CAMP lavas flowed near the time of the Triassic-Jurassic extinction. The lavas of the Deccan Traps flowed at the K-T, or Cretaceous-Tertiary boundary, when the extinction that marks the end of the dinosaur age occurred.

Were they merely coincidental or did LIPs play a role in the extinctions? No one is sure. Greg hopes to find out. In the meantime, he has a hunch that they did. He imagines that LIPs could have caused catastrophic change in much the same way a bolide impact may have, by spewing large quantities of toxins high into the atmosphere.

"The most likely scenario," Greg wrote in a scientific paper, "involves the injection into the upper atmosphere of large amounts of sulfur dioxide and carbon dioxide, causing drastic, if temporary climatic cooling followed by heating." He believes that high lava fountains could easily have sent super hot gases and chemicals into the upper atmosphere where they would quickly circle the globe. The result would be similar to a bolide impact and could produce global climatic change severe enough to cause massive extinctions.

That's not to say that a bolide strike couldn't be followed by massive volcanism. It may even be that bolide impacts have contributed to or caused periods of volcanism. It could be that several of the greatest extinctions of the past coincided not only with lava floods, but also followed the impact of a large meteor— and that a combination of factors must be considered causal, rather than any one in particular.

Over the boundary: A different world

"Go over the Triassic-Jurassic boundary and the path toward dinosaur diversity seems relatively slow, but it looks inexorable," Paul observes. "That is, you start off with more and more and more kinds of dinosaurs that become more and more and more diverse.

"The things that become abundant after all these other things disappear are dinosaurs and crocodilians," he continues. "Mammals survive, as well. Dinosaurs and mammals evolved about the same time in the Triassic and they both survived the Triassic-Jurassic extinction."

The world the survivors inherited was a changed place. Where there had been many different kinds of plants and animals before the catastrophe, there were suddenly far fewer forms of living things. The variety of "floral provinces" Paul and his colleagues described from the Late Triassic was gone. Natural communities around the globe were less diverse and more alike. The terrestrial fauna, or land-dwelling animals, were greatly changed. Not only were tetrapods suddenly less diverse, the reptiles of the Early Jurassic were different from reptiles of the Late Triassic.

The Connecticut Valley in the Early Jurassic

Life made its recovery in the Connecticut Valley along the shallows of the many large lakes that existed. Much of what we know about the Connecticut Valley in the Early Jurassic has been learned from footprints left along these lakeshores. Today they provide a record of survivor communities as they were about 600,000 years after the Triassic-Jurassic extinction.

Lake levels rose and fell according to the seasons. The climate in the valley in the Early Jurassic alternated between long dry seasons and shorter rainy seasons. These were in turn influenced by the gravitational pull other planets exerted on the earth's axis, following cycles Paul has described as "grand seasons." Grand seasons function over much longer periods of time than a year— from tens of thousands to millions of years—and continue to influence weather patterns today.

Extensive shallows along the lakeshores supported a variety of plants, including primitive ferns and seed plants, cycads, gingkos and the conifers that came to dominate the land. It's possible some early flowering plants had evolved by then, but they would have been few and far between.

There were insects similar in form to cockroaches, beetles, crickets or grasshoppers, cicadas or aphids, lacewings and

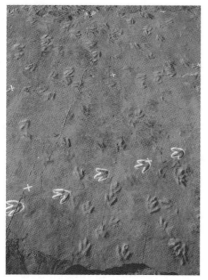

dragonflies or damselflies. Fish were also plentiful. Besides dinosaurs, the Connecticut Valley is also famous for preserving abundant fossil fish. Several families are known from the Early Jurassic, including *Semionotus*, *Ptycholepis*, *Redfieldius* and the large coelacanth *Diplurus longicaudatus*, a predator that ate other fish whole. The lakes also likely supported varieties of freshwater clams and shrimp, as well as various algae.

The valley's terrestrial fauna (land-dwelling animals) was different from that which existed in the Late Triassic. Many reptiles, such as *Erpetosuchus*, *Hypsognathus* and *Stegomus*, along with phytosaurs like *Rutiodon*, disappeared. New forms of dinosaurs appeared for the first time.

Hypsognathus

Small theropods like those that appeared in the Late Triassic expanded. They are joined almost immediately by new and much larger theropods. Their tracks indicate that they prowled the valley's lakeshores in large numbers, hungrily scarfing up anything that moved.

Prosauropod dinosaurs, possibly primitive sauropod dinosaurs, and new forms of ornithischian dinosaurs also appeared. Presumably, the herbivores made only brief visits to the lakeshores, preferring to graze in the forest understory and stay out of the way of the theropods.

Bob Baron's Frisbee

How do paleontologists find the fossils that enable them to draw such fantastic conclusions? Sometimes they get help from amateurs—people who find things that grab their curiosity—like Bob and Jim Baron and their friend, David Bazzano. As kids, these men found a specimen of *Hypsognathus*, a rare example of one of the primitive reptiles Paul says lived in the Late Triassic and went extinct around the Triassic-Jurassic boundary. The fossil they found while playing Frisbee in 1967 is now a key piece of evidence that helps support Paul's theory.

"The reality is, that the finding was pure luck," Bob recalled in a letter he wrote to the collection manager at the Yale Peabody Museum in 1996. Nearly thirty years earlier, Bob, then 7; his brother Jim, 6; and their friend, David Bazzano, 12, found a fossil that earned them a trip to New Haven and special thanks from the Peabody's curators, John Ostrom and Elwyn Simons. "As a little boy, in the second grade," Bob wrote, "I really didn't have a clue as to the significance of 'the rock.' Luckily enough, my friend David was beginning to study dinosaurs and fossils in his classes."

The rock the boys found in the stone wall behind the Baron's backyard in Meriden, Connecticut, contained a fossil skull and a cast of the skeleton of *Hypsognathus fenneri*, an ancient form of reptile known as a procolophonid. It's one of the most anatomically primitive reptiles known and, according to Paul, an example of a group that went extinct at the Triassic-Jurassic boundary.

"Anyway, my brother, David, and myself were out playing Frisbee in the back yard, and David threw the toy over my head. It landed on top of an old stonewall. In my haste to get the Frisbee,

David Bazzano & the Baron brothers show off the fossil they found for Peabody curators John Ostrom (left) and Elwyn Simons.
Courtesy of the Peabody Museum of Natural History, Yale University, New Haven, CT

I stumbled on the wall, dislodging a large rock. When I went to put it back, and had trouble lifting it, David came over to help. He noticed the imprints on the rock, and began to tell me about fossils. We wanted to show it to my mother, so we both carried it up to the house. Apparently, and luckily enough, she was intrigued by this fossil. I guess she wanted us to learn about what we had found, and started making phone calls. The rest of the story you already know."

The rock was a ten-pound piece of red sandstone. What the boys saw was a natural mold of its backbones, ribs and forelimbs. Locked inside was a fine skull, better preserved and more complete than any other specimen known from North America. It was chiseled free of the sandstone by Peabody Museum fossil preparator Peter Whybrow and paleontologist Bob Bakker, at that time an undergraduate student at Yale.

Debating the past with an eye toward the future

Paul's work in the valley has also helped make his theory for the expansion of the dinosaurs a hot topic among paleontologists. There are several different opinions as to how dinosaurs came to live so well and for so long, and the role extinctions may or may not have played in their success—but the debate reaches even further.

However things unfolded, events in the Late Triassic and Early Jurassic shaped the world we know today. It wasn't just dinosaurs that evolved during the Triassic. Humans trace their roots back that far as well, to when early mammals appeared. Many paleontologists believe that understanding this time in the ancient past—around the Triassic-Jurassic boundary—may be vital to anticipating our future.

As humans, we are what biologists refer to as terrestrial vertebrates (land-dwelling animals built around a backbone). To anatomists we're tetrapods (vertebrates with four feet or limbs). That puts us, along with dinosaurs, crocodiles and turtles, in a large group of animals that appeared in the Triassic and survive in one form or another today (birds being the survivors of dinosaurs).

We're here today because our ancestors survived the Late Triassic and Early Jurassic when other forms of life went extinct. What makes things interesting today is that we're witnessing another mass extinction, perhaps the greatest ever.

"Not only are we in the midst of one," says paleontologist Spencer Lucas, "but it's the big one. This one's going to make the end-Permian extinction look like a walk in the park. It will be over in a few thousand years—and you may not even have to wait that long."

The question is, who will survive? What will the world look like the day after? Where will life go next? We know time eventually ran out for life's "big body experiment," the dinosaurs. Few can look at current rates of decline in global biodiversity and not wonder where this extinction will leave humans, nature's "big brain experiment."

If there is an answer to this great debate in paleontology at the beginning of the twenty-first century, it may lie in the sandstone layers of the Connecticut Valley, where paleontology in the New World got its start two centuries ago.

Scientific debate and the Triassic-Jurassic boundary

"The old joke is that if you put two geologists in a room together you'll get an argument," Rich Krueger says with a chuckle. And, of course, that's the whole point. "That's all science is," says Spencer Lucas. "Good science is debate. It's anarchistic and arrogant. No sooner do new ideas come than other scientists—if the process is working—challenge these ideas based on their data or assumptions or different methods."

The debates surrounding the expansion of the dinosaurs and the Triassic-Jurassic extinction are no exceptions. There are several different points of view as to exactly what happened, each passionately argued by its leading proponent.

"This is a really hot topic right now," Spencer says. "I think in a few years we're going to know a lot more and that's exciting." Spencer, Paul, and English paleontologist Mike Benton have all advocated different views of extinctions and the roles they may have played in contributing to the success of dinosaurs.

Paul advocates the theory that a single mass extinction, at the Triassic-Jurassic boundary, set dinosaurs on the path to success. It's Mike Benton's view that the door was opened for dinosaurs long before, by an earlier extinction, before the end of the Triassic. For his part, Spencer Lucas thinks both his colleagues' accounts of extinctions are overstated. He isn't convinced extinctions had anything to do with dinosaurs' survival.

For now, it's anyone's guess as to who is right. "Maybe we'll know in a few years," Spencer says, "but that doesn't matter. What matters is that we're trying to find out what's right. One thing for sure is that the earth has a unique history. We're all trying to discover the history. That's our goal. We just want to figure out what happened."

Mike Benton's two-step theory of dinosaur evolution

"It seems to me that the radiation of the dinosaurs is a two-step process," says Mike Benton, Professor of Vertebrate Paleontology at the University of Bristol, England. He believes dinosaurs were beginning to grow larger and more diverse twenty or thirty million years before the Triassic-Jurassic boundary.

"I think you have difficulty looking at what we know of the Connecticut Valley, with abundant dinosaur footprints in the Late Triassic, [and] saying that somehow the dinosaurs had not yet radiated, [when] they're making footprints all over the place. I think that there was indeed a piece of extinction at about the Carnian-Norian boundary [roughly 25 million years before the Triassic-Jurassic boundary] and the Triassic-Jurassic boundary was the second event. I think the end-Carnian event was bigger."

"That was the major change," Mike says. "That was the beginning of all these groups. It's not just the dinosaurs. It's the pterosaurs and the pre-lizards and mammals and all of those. All of that was happening back down there [in the Late Triassic] and they were all still around after the boundary, the turtles and the mammals and the lizards and the crocodiles and the dinosaurs, all of them went through. The only things that went out on land at the end of the Triassic were the rauisuchians, the phytosaurs, three or four groups of top carnivores. The difference was not that great. Top carnivores go out and the dinosaurs diversify further. And I'm not sure why Paul keeps shoving the emphasis the way that he does. The facts speak against it."

Paul Olsen's point of view

The essential thing for Paul is to know precisely how old the fossils you base your findings on really are. He's not satisfied that Mike's data holds up to that sort of scrutiny. "Whatever [fossils] define [Benton's] mass extinction is not the age that he thinks it is," Paul says, "and worse than that they're scattered. They're different ages, what Spencer Lucas would call the 'compiled correlation effect.'

"The compiled correlation effect is what happens when people base their work on the literature and [stop] going out and looking at real rocks and fossils," Spencer explains, referring to scientific articles published in paleontology journals. "What ends up happening is that extinction events get artificially concentrated at the beginnings or ends of time intervals."

It's Paul's position that the evidence he's gathered in the Connecticut Valley and other rift valleys of eastern North America is more reliable. The unique geology of the rift valleys makes it possible to date fossils more precisely and give a more accurate accounting of when various animal species or taxa go extinct.

"A lot of the taxa [Benton] claims go extinct at the Carnian-Norian boundary in fact go right through it and go extinct at the Triassic-Jurassic boundary," Paul says. "A good example is a genus supposedly restricted to the Carnian called *Erpetosuchus*. We found it in Connecticut in Norian [later] rocks. Another example were cynodonts that were supposed to go extinct at the Carnian-Norian boundary. They are also known from Norian deposits."

Erpetosuchus: **What a croc!**

As the story goes, Paul was on a geology field trip to Cheshire, Connecticut, in March 1995 when he noticed a "white blob" on the ground—but there were a lot of other white blobs in the soil as well. He kept walking at first, but his famous fossil senses must have started tingling because he stopped to look more closely. When he did he found a fossil tooth—one unlike any found in North America before. After digging further, he was rewarded with the discovery of the skull that went with it, that of an approximately 212 million-year-old archosaur, an ancient crocodile relative. The only other fossil like it was found in Scotland a century before. Named *Erpetosuchus*, it was about the size of a house cat, with long legs thin enough that it may have been able to run at a gallop.

The find was more than just spectacularly unlikely or fantastically serendipitous; it was just the sort of clue Paul has spent his life searching to uncover. Finding *Erpetosuchus* in Connecticut established a new link between fossils found in Europe and those found in the Connecticut Valley. Because the ages of the rocks of the Connecticut Valley are so well known, Paul was able to determine the age of the fossil very precisely. He based his conclusion on at least three different methods of scientific analyses. Each technique gave a similar result: the fossil was between 210 and 214 million years old.

Restoration of Erpetosuchus by Paul E. Olsen
Courtesy, Paul E. Olsen

The result showed that *Erpetosuchus* lived for tens of millions of years longer than previously thought. Instead of going extinct at the end of the Carnian stage of the Late Triassic, as Mike Benton stated, at least one was still alive in Cheshire ten million years later, during the Norian stage near the end of the Triassic Period. Of course, *Erpetosuchus* would still have had another ten million years or so to go for it to survive until the Triassic-Jurassic boundary, as Paul believes it did.

That's the way things are in paleontology. Fossil evidence and other data take knowledge only so far; the rest is left to theorists. Answers are seldom clear-cut. The most even the experts can do is make their best guess, based on everything they've learned and their best fossil sense, until their ideas can be put to some sort of test or compared with a newly discovered bit of evidence. Sometimes you get lucky and sometimes you make your own luck.

Spencer Lucas's point of view

"I think the extinction event at the end of the Carnian has been greatly overstated," Spencer Lucas observes, "and the same is true of the extinction at the end of the Triassic. I think what there was between those points in time were intervals of relatively high extinction rates and that there were two or more extinctions between the Carnian and the end of the Triassic. I'm not sure, though, that those extinctions, however you interpret them, had much to do with the success of the dinosaurs.

"I think dinosaurian success is based on being a dinosaur in the kind of world where being a dinosaur is advantageous. They evolve as animals that are relatively small and active. That's what sets them apart, so they come into a world where being small, upright and active gives them an advantage. "You have to remember this took millions of years. I don't see it as them outcompeting other animals; that's silly. I see it as a much more lengthy, gradual process of adapting to changing circumstances.

"As far as I'm concerned, Benton's ideas were refuted years ago, not just by me, but by Paul and everybody else who critiqued them. I think Paul is closer to right, because I think what happens when you go from the Triassic into the Jurassic is way more—way more— significant than what happened at the end of the Carnian.

"The place Paul and I differ is simply this: Paul wants to believe there was a single extinction at the very end of the Triassic and that reset everything. I don't think the fossil record supports that. I think what it supports is that there was an accelerated interval of extinction. There were all these changes happening in the Late Triassic and they were finally culminated when we get into the Jurassic, rather than, boom, it just happening all at once."

The evidence

Science is a process of coming up with ideas and then proving them true or false. It's based on gaining experience—and Paul's experience searching the rift valleys of eastern North America is unrivaled. His idea of a mass extinction at the Triassic-Jurassic boundary has itself been formed over time, shaped by his observations and the analyses he's made of the information.

In recent years, he's collected a large amount of information from 70 locations associated with the rift valleys up and down eastern North America, from New Brunswick to the Carolinas. He's mapped and measured fossil footprints and bones of dinosaurs and of nondinosaurs. He's fine-tuned when animals appear and disappear in the fossil record. He's compared sizes and numbers and gauged the overall diversity of their communities.

He's also kept track of what was going on with the local environment. Paul and his colleagues have checked for what are known as telltale signs of ecological catastrophes, of bolide impacts and of LIP's. They have looked for what are known as fern spikes (evidence of severe disruption of plant communities) and for the presence of rare minerals and elements that are markers of bolide impacts. They have combed through sediments to see when lava flowed.

It seems like a great deal of evidence, but none of it would be worth much if not for one more, critical measure: Time. In this case, time is on his side—one of the things Paul loves most about East Coast rift valleys.

Controlling time

Few places in the world can rival the valley for the way it precisely recorded events in the deep past. Paul has learned to use its quirks as a sort of chronograph to time events around the Triassic-Jurassic boundary with previously unheard-of precision.

"The footprints are extremely abundant in strata that have superb time control," Paul explains. "This is very different from what you see in other paleontological realms. It's not an exaggeration to say that we can sample a record of these animals at a very fine timescale, potentially less than 20,000 years per sample, and we get a picture of changes in diversity that is extremely high resolution compared to what is usual in paleontology."

Grand seasons

The sediments recorded time by tracking seasonal climatic changes. Seasons of heavy rains scoured large amounts of sand and gravel from the highlands, depositing sediment in the valley in thick wet layers commonly known as "red beds" and recognized by their rust red color. Thinner grey sediments record cycles of change from wetter to drier seasons. The darkest gray layers are sediments that settled to the bottom of deep lakes where a lack of oxygen prevented grains of iron ores from turning the rust red color of the red beds.

After searching the ground, Paul and his colleagues scanned the heavens to find a way to precisely measure the age of these different layers. What he found was that the earth is something like the pendulum in a cosmic grandfather clock, being pulled back and forth by the orbits of nearby planets. "We think of the annual cycle as the only seasonal change we see," Paul explains, "but that's not really true. Sediments record extremely high frequency and fine-scaled climatic cycles stemming from changes in the orientation of the earth's orbit caused by gravitational attraction of the planets and the moon.

"They're like 'grand seasons.' Our annual cycle is due to the earth's orbit relative to the plane in which it moves around the sun. There are other cycles that have time periods that are vastly longer than a year, namely, tens of thousands of years to millions of years. But, like the annual cycle, they influence the environment and the way sediments are laid down—and that's recorded in the rock record."

Calibrating the age of different sediments using grand seasons has provided Paul with a measure of absolute time that he uses to date everything he has discovered within them. By counting up or down layers of sediment, Paul has been able to isolate when different fossils found in the valley appeared and disappeared—and more accurately than can be done most anywhere else on earth. Together, the fossils recount events that are consistent with Paul's theory of extinction at the Triassic-Jurassic boundary and the expansion of the dinosaurs. His theory is compelling, if not conclusive.

The footprints

Fossil footprints have the unique quality of being not just fossils, but also geologic features. There is no doubt that a footprint is the same age as the layer of rock it's found in. Based on the level of precision with which Paul has come to understand the age of local sediments, he's been able to determine when various trackmakers left their marks.

His reviews of the Connecticut Valley footprints, as well as of fossil bones, give a remarkable account of the changes in terrestrial animal groups (known as the "tetrapod transition") at the Triassic-Jurassic boundary. The footprints give clear evidence that early ornithischian dinosaurs and theropod dinosaurs survived into the Jurassic, while many other forms of reptiles did not.

Also intriguing is the sudden appearance of *Eubrontes*, the footprint Hitchcock dubbed "true thunder," very shortly after the boundary. Theropods apparently suddenly grew much larger and more dangerous in the earliest Jurassic, perhaps in response to the elimination of large, nondinosaurian carnivores such as *Postosuchus*. Prosauropods also appeared in tropical regions of Pangaea for the first time, as evidenced by footprints known as *Otozoum*.

It's also possible that large theropods like those that made the footprint *Eubrontes*, migrated to the valley following an environmental disruption, a prospect Spencer Lucas has raised, but that possibility, along with so many others in paleontology, remains undetermined.

Fern spikes

Besides animal fossils, there are a couple of other key pieces of evidence Paul and his colleagues have extracted from rift valley sediments. Bruce Cornet has worked with Paul for years to examine fossil plants commonly found in East Coast rift valleys. Ferns have been of special interest because they can provide evidence of environmental disruptions.

After the eruption of Mt. St. Helens, for example, ferns were among the first plants to reestablish themselves on the barren mountainsides left after the volcanic explosion. Spores can travel great distances and ferns are known to produce higher levels of spores in response to times of environmental stress, two reasons they are able to quickly colonize areas like the ground around active volcanoes. Palynologists (scientists who study fossil spores and pollen) like Bruce look at the relative levels of fern spores preserved in sediments as a means of identifying times of environmental stress in the past.

What Paul's colleague Sarah Fowell found in looking at the rift valleys was a higher than expected proportion of ferns and fern spores present in sediments associated with the Triassic-Jurassic boundary. Paul and Sarah concluded that the plants were responding to environmental stress, most probably the same stress that caused extinction to occur.

The iridium anomaly

Another key piece of evidence turned up during Paul's search of the sediments, in the form of a very rare element. He and several colleagues found the element iridium in the rift valley sediments of the Newark Basin of New Jersey. Iridium is normally present only at extremely low levels on earth but has been associated with asteroids and meteorites. It is one element whose presence is considered a telltale sign of the presence of meteor remnants in terrestrial rock.

Paul reported finding higher than expected levels of iridium, or an iridium anomaly, in a paper he published in 2002. His results showed that the anomaly coincided with Bruce Cornet's fern spike, suggesting a bolide impact at the Triassic-Jurassic boundary and adding support to his theory of the extinction.

The future

Two important pieces of evidence still remain to be found before Paul will know if he's right in his view of events around the Triassic-Jurassic boundary—or not. In addition to his search for an impact crater, Paul is also interested in finding evidence of a rare mineral known as "shocked quartz" that might exist at or near the boundary. Shocked quartz is formed under extreme heat and pressure, like that which would occur with an asteroid impact. Evidence of it would further bolster the notion of an impact causing a global environmental disaster.

While results Paul has so far obtained are consistent with his theory, more remains to be done before he can conclusively state his theory for the expansion of the dinosaurs.

The Dinosaurs   8

The Connecticut Valley theropod dinosaur Podokesaurus, by Will Sillin.

T he dinosaurs of the Connecticut Valley are known today
from a sort of composite sketch. What is known has been
learned mostly from footprints, relatively few skeletons and
even fewer natural casts. The rest has been filled in by comparisons
to dinosaurs known to have lived at about the same time elsewhere,
and by more than a little bit of imagination.

Dogs & cats

Paleontologists are still not sure exactly which species of dinosaurs made individual footprints—and they may never be. Instead they refer to local dinosaurs in terms of the families of dinosaurs that footprints most likely represent.

"We talk about trackmakers in a broad sense, the same way we talk about cats and dogs," Paul explains. "For example, when you're in Africa there are several kinds of cats. That's the level at which we can distinguish [Connecticut Valley dinosaurs]: cats and dogs. You can't tell [beagles from bulldogs]. The only way you would be able to tell [dinosaurs] apart by footprints would be if you already knew what species made which footprints."

"During the Early Jurassic, the carnivorous dinosaurs really looked similar to one another," Paul continues. "Some of them may have had bigger crests on the head, but the body forms are really, really similar, so much so that if you just have the feet you can't tell them apart. We could have had many different species of dinosaur that were identical except for their heads, pretty much the same kind of animal—we don't know.

"In that sense," Paul explains, "we know there were theropod dinosaurs, similar to *Podokesaurus* and *Dilophosaurus*. *Podokesaurus* may have made *Grallator* and *Anchisauripus*, and *Dilophosaurus* may have made *Eubrontes*. Then you have herbivorous dinosaurs, of which there are two flavors. There were small ornithischian dinosaurs that looked like *Lesothosaurus* that would have made *Anomoepus*. They were considerably smaller than the carnivores. The largest had a hip height of about three feet. Most were turkey sized. And then you had the prosauropods, *Anchisaurus* and *Ammosaurus*, and they made *Otozoum*."

The Connecticut Valley Dinosaurs

Ichnological Evidence *Footprints known from the Connecticut Valley*	Osteological Correlates *Dinosaurs known from bones that may have been similar to the valley's trackmakers*
Grallator *Eubrontes*	**Theropod Dinosaurs** *Podokesaurus?* *Coelophysis?* *Dilophosaurus?* *Syntarsus?*
Otozoum	**Prosauropod Dinosaurs** *Anchisaurus?* *Ammosaurus?*
Anomoepus	**Ornithischian Dinosaurs** *Lesothosaurus?* *Scutellosaurus?*

The major groups

Saurischian & ornithischian dinosaurs

In 1988, dinosaurs were classified by the English paleontologist Harry Seely into two major groups or orders based on features of their hips. Early forms known from the Connecticut Valley included dinosaurs belonging to each of these orders, the saurischians and ornithischians.

The prosauropods and theropods were both early forms of saurischian dinosaurs. They are known from both fossil bone and footprint evidence. The footprint known as *Anomoepus* provides the only evidence of ornithischian dinosaurs.

Saurischian dinosaurs

The theropods

Connecticut Valley theropods were generalists—meat-eaters that would sink their teeth into anything. Footprints show theropods dominated the valley in the Early Jurassic and came in at least two sizes, small and medium, compared to later theropods like *Tyrannosaurus rex*.

The theropods walked and ran on two feet. The larger version may have been able to run at seven to ten miles per hour. They moved with their feet close to the center lines of their bodies, suggesting they were thin and quick. Few impressions of their forefeet have been found. This suggests that their forefeet were small, as was often the case in theropods.

Theropods had curved necks like modern-day herons and cranes, birds now thought to be their descendants. They also had long tails. Smaller versions, like *Podokesaurus*, were roughly three to six feet long with snakelike heads and long, thin, hind legs. Larger theropods were up to 20 feet long, with thick, stout, hind legs and big heads bearing substantial jawbones. All had snouts filled with long, daggerlike teeth well suited for penetrating hides and tearing flesh.

The prosauropods

Prosauropod dinosaurs were early forms of plant-eaters. They were among the first to feature long necks, long tails and capacious bellies—a body style that reached enormous proportions in later sauropod dinosaurs such as *Apatosaurus.*

Two dinosaurs known from the valley, *Anchisaurus* and *Ammosaurus,* have been identified as prosauropods. Paleontologist Adam Yates has argued they may even have been early sauropods. In either case, they would be among the smallest and most primitive prosauropods or sauropods. These dinosaurs walked on two legs, occasionally dropping down on all fours. *Anchisaurus* was roughly five to eight feet in length. *Ammosaurus* was similar, but perhaps larger—roughly 12 to 15 feet long.

"Prosauropods were the first herbivorous radiation of dinosaurs," explains Peter Galton. "With their long necks they reached up fairly high for food. A third of the animal is neck, which meant they could reach higher than ornithischians. They led in a similar direction to sauropods when they went really high."

Prosauropods lacked the heavy-duty grinding teeth later plant-eaters developed. The saw-edged teeth of the valley's prosauropods suggests they may have favored softer leaves that required less crushing and grinding. "I think the model [of a prosauropod] at Dinosaur State Park is pretty good," observes Peter. "They've got cheeks which is nice. Cheeks are functionally important for a plant-eater. They can't keep their food in without them."

Ornithischian dinosaurs

Ornithischian dinosaurs grew to be the more numerous of the two orders and included many fantastic forms. Early ornithischians, likely represented by the footprint *Anomoepus,* were forerunners of many bizarre-looking dinosaurs such as *Stegosaurus, Triceratops* and the duckbill, *Hadrosaurus,* which thrived in Late Jurassic and Cretaceous times. The primitive ornithischian was turkey sized, with a long neck, relatively long legs and round belly.

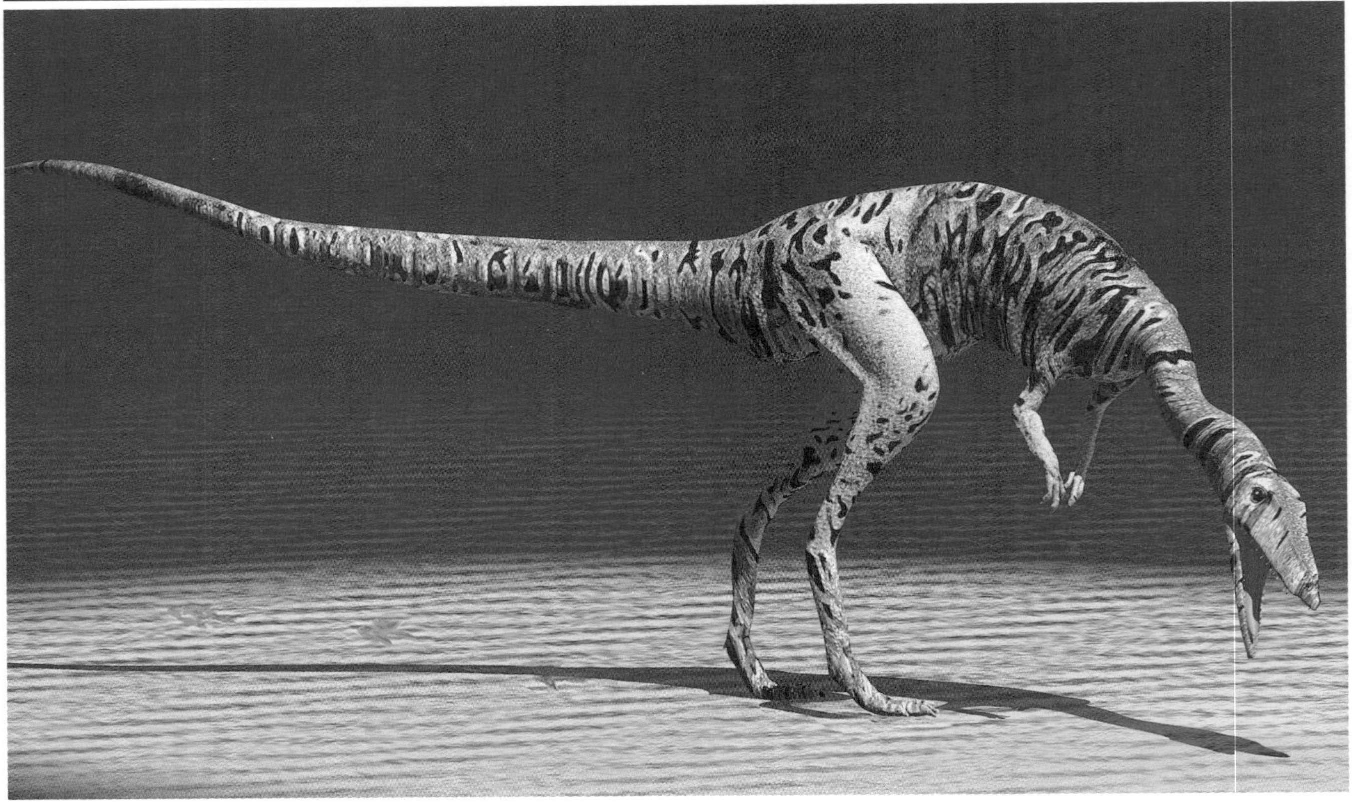

The Connecticut Valley theropod dinosaur *Podokesaurus*, by Will Sillin.

Theropod Bone Discoveries in the Valley

The Bones from Fort Adams
Coelophysis
"hollow form"
Cast of natural cast of bones
(Boston Society of Natural History 13656)
YPM 3912 (cast)
Quarried: Middletown, Connecticut
Discovered: Fort Adams,
Newport, Rhode Island
1864

Theropod Tooth
Coelophysis
on display at Dinosaur State Park, CT

The Bones from Holyoke
Podokesaurus holyokensis (Coelophysis holyokensis)
"swift-footed lizard"
Cast of partial skeleton
(original specimen destroyed by fire)
YPM 314 (cast)
S. Hadley, Massachusetts
1864

Grallator cursorius
Amherst College No. 4/1
(from Lull, 1953).
Courtesy, Connecticut Department of
Environmental Protection

Grallator trackway
(from Lull, 1953).
Courtesy, Connecticut Department of
Environmental Protection

Theropod footprints in the valley
Grallator, "one who goes on stilts"
Edward Hitchcock, 1858

Grallator is the footprint of a small theropod or several kinds of small theropods. Some were perhaps no bigger than turkeys, but the valley's smaller theropod dinosaur would have presented a far more intimidating countenance than any barnyard fowl.

They were likely swift and agile predators, remarkable for their relatively long legs and stride.

"Some of the birds had extremely long legs," Hitchcock wrote of the trackmakers, "and I have arranged them under the genus *Grallator*...The stride of the *Grallator cursorius* [the racer] was 24 inches—very long for a bird of that size."

The *Grallator* footprint was probably made by dinosaurs that walked and ran on two legs and made footprints between three to six inches long and perhaps longer. They moved with their feet close beneath them and only a few inches apart, suggestive of a theropod.

The trackmaker may have been similar to *Podokesaurus*, the small theropod known from bones discovered in South Hadley, Massachusetts, or *Coelophysis*, the small theropod known to have lived during Triassic time.

Grallator footprints exist in a wide range of sizes, leading Paul Olsen to wonder if some of the smallest theropod footprints found in the valley might not have been made by theropod babies and juveniles.

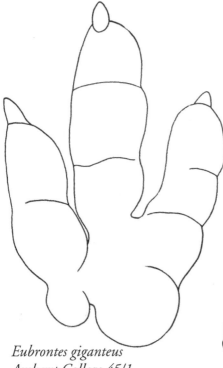

*Eubrontes trackway
(from Lull, 1953).*
Courtesy, Connecticut Department of
Environmental Protection

*Eubrontes giganteus
Amherst College 45/1
(from Lull, 1953).*
Courtesy, Connecticut Department of
Environmental Protection

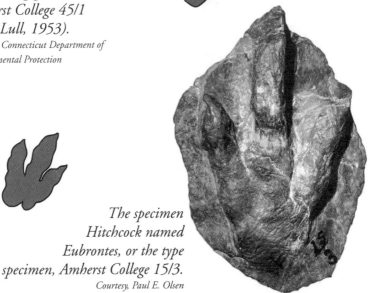

*The specimen
Hitchcock named
Eubrontes, or the type
specimen, Amherst College 15/3.*
Courtesy, Paul E. Olsen

Theropod footprints in the valley
Eubrontes, "true thunder"
Edward Hitchcock, 1858

The footprint known as *Eubrontes* was made by a theropod dinosaur perhaps 20 feet long. Large compared to other dinosaurs in the valley, the trackmaker was a middleweight compared to Cretaceous theropods such as *Tyrannosaurus rex.*

The exact nature of the trackmaker is open to debate, but it walked on two legs and made footprints between 12 and 18 inches long. It may have been like *Dilophosaurus,* a theropod from the Early Jurassic known from skeletons in Arizona. Paleontologist Rob Weems has suggested *Eubrontes* may instead be the track of a prosauropod. Hypotheses that the tracks are those of an early reptile similar to *Herrerasaurus* or a prosauropod such as *Plateosaurus* have been proposed, and are still under review.

Eubrontes tracks were among the most common in the valley and a favorite of Hitchcock's: "First come that huge giant, *Brontozoum giganteum* [a name he gave the footprints after *Eubrontes*] with a foot 18 inches long and embracing an area 13 inches square within its outlines. Its stride was from [2-1/2 to five feet] and its legs were so long that it went forward nearly on a straight line. The great resemblance between the...foot [and that of the Rhea] make it probable that this was the great courser [great war horse] of sandstone days."

Hitchcock sometimes used water to measure footprints, with astonishing results. "One from Northampton, No. 15/1, will hold four quarts of water," he noted. He also wondered if they moved in groups. "It appears that these enormous birds passed over the surface in flocks, as their rows of tracks, near the railroad in the south-east part of Northampton, show...How amazed should we be to meet flocks of such birds now."

The footprint was designated the State Fossil in 1991 at the request of Connecticut school children.

157

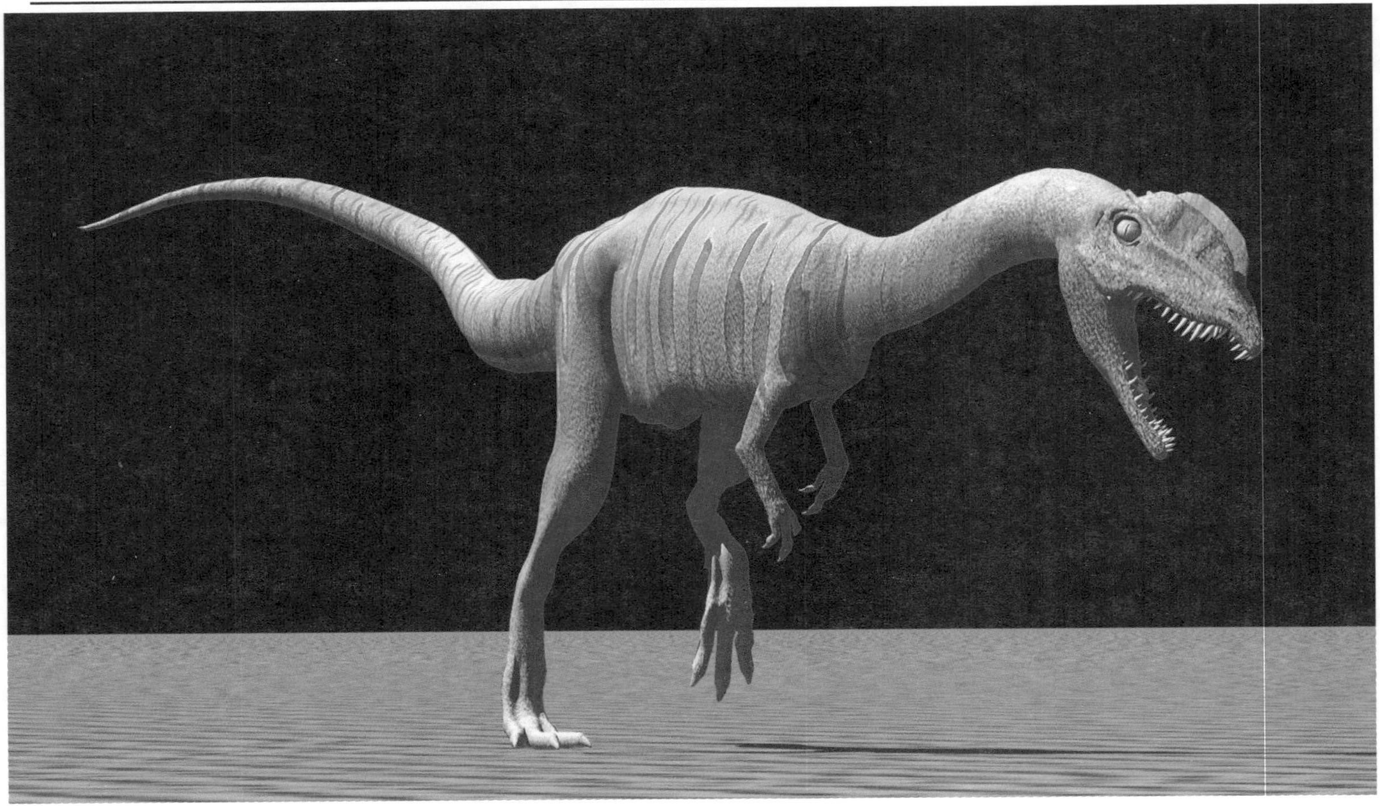

The theropod dinosaur known from Arizona, *Dilophosaurus*, by Will Sillin.

Possible *Eubrontes* Trackmaker

Dilophosaurus wetherilli
"double-crested lizard"
Theropod dinosaur
Multiple skeletons
Early Jurassic
Discovered: Kayenta Formation, Arizona
1942

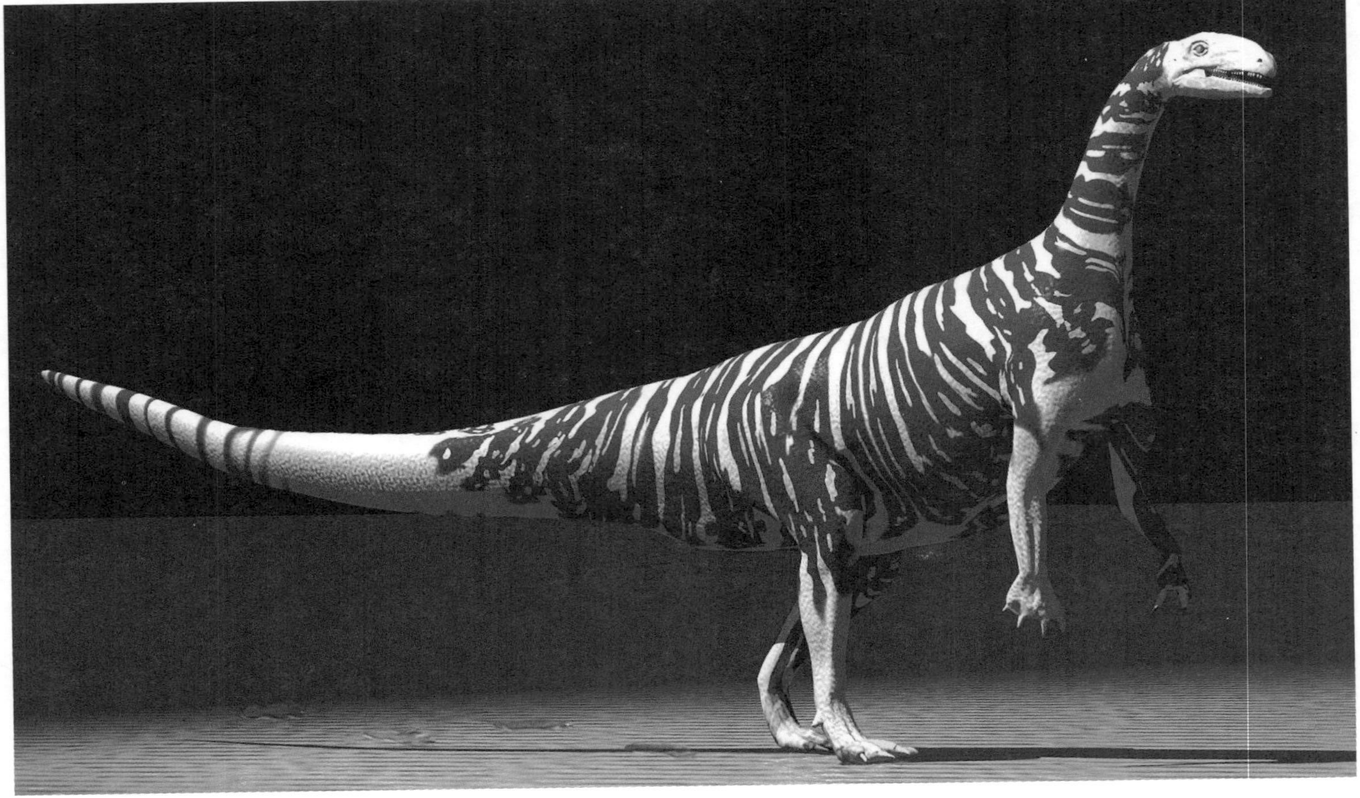

A Connecticut Valley prosauropod dinosaur similar to *Anchisaurus*, by Will Sillin.

Prosauropod Bone Discoveries in the Valley

"The Bones from the Well"
Indeterminate prosauropod
Partial skeleton
YPM 2125
East Windsor, Connecticut
1818

"The Bones from the Armory"
Anchisaurus polyzelus
"near lizard"
Partial skeleton
Amherst College 41/109-118
Springfield, Massachusetts
1855

"The Bones from the Bridge"
Ammosaurus major
"sand lizard"
Partial skeleton
YPM 208
Manchester, Connecticut
1884

"The Quarry Bones II"
Anchisaurus polyzelus
Partial skeleton, once known as
Yaleosaurus, of a juvenile.
YPM 1883
Manchester, Connecticut
1891

"The Quarry Bones III"
Ammosaurus major
Partial skeleton
YPM 209
Manchester, Connecticut
1891

Note: In 2004, Adam Yates argued
that "The Bones from the Bridge"
(YPM 208) and the Quarry Bones III
(YPM 209) are both the same species
of plant-eating dinosaur, *Anchisaurus
polyzelus*, an early sauropod.

*Otozoum moodii
Amherst College No. 4/1
(from Lull, 1953).*
Courtesy, Connecticut Department of
Environmental Protection

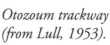

*Otozoum trackway
(from Lull, 1953).*
Courtesy, Connecticut Department of
Environmental Protection

Prosauropod footprints in the valley

Otozoum, "giant animal"

Edward Hitchcock, 1847

Edward Hitchcock described *Otozoum* as the "most extraordinary track yet brought to light in this valley . . . distinguished from all others" by the massive appearance of its footprints. It lumbered along taking steps perhaps just 2-1/2 feet long with its feet spread nearly as far apart, suggesting it had the build of a big-bellied plant-eater. It walked mostly on two legs but made occasional impressions of its five-toed hands, complete with claws.

"So peculiar is the shape of the track," noted Hitchcock, "that I should hardly have dared describe it from a single specimen." One aspect of its tracks which intrigued Hitchcock was what he believed was webbing between the toes. "Beneath this foot. . . was a web, as I have reason to suppose, which, like a great snow shoe, kept the animal from sinking deep into the mud. And yet its feet did sink at least two inches. . . I incline to the opinion that such an animal as [made] the *Otozoum* had the power of walking on two feet or four feet; and in fact did rarely use the fore feet, save when wishing to bring its head to the ground."

Lull later wrote that the webbing Hitchcock described was instead the result of a wave of mud being pushed out from beneath the dinosaur's foot under its great weight. Hitchcock also imagined *Otozoum* to be the track of an enormous animal, as anyone might from the size of its footprints, but Paul Olsen says the footprints give a false impression. "*Otozoum* tracks are tricky," warns Paul, "because they look like they are much bigger than they really are. The difference is that the *Otozoum* foot implants not just the toes, but all the way up to the ankle. The footprint is as big as *Eubrontes*, but if you scaled it to the same part of the foot as *Eubrontes* it wouldn't be as big, so the animal wasn't very big."

163

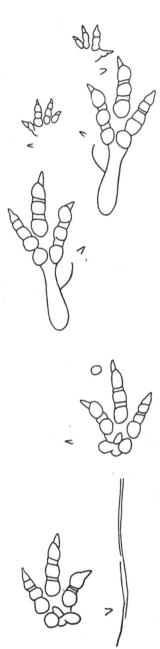

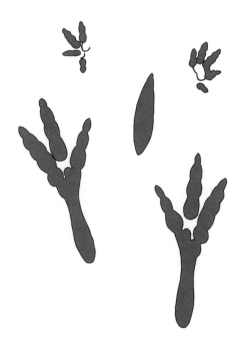

*Anomoepus trackway
(from Lull, 1953).*
Courtesy, Connecticut Department of
Environmental Protection

*Anomoepus scambus
Amherst College No. 16/5
Sitting impression
(from Lull, 1953).*
Courtesy, Connecticut Department of
Environmental Protection

Ornithischian footprints in the valley
Anomoepus, "unlike foot"
Edward Hitchcock, 1858

The footprint *Anomoepus* is known perhaps as much for the impressions of hands as rear feet. Hitchcock gave it its name, meaning "unlike foot," because of the puzzling appearance of its forefeet, or hands, compared with its rear feet.

Impressions of the rear feet were much like a turkey's, but often accompanied by smaller, five-toed impressions of its forefeet. The question Hitchcock pondered looking at them was how could a bird have hands?

And then there were the sitting traces, made when the trackmaker rested on the ground, that suggested a different animal altogether. "Indeed, they look very much like the tracks of a large dog," Hitchcock wrote.

Paul says the handprints are a sure sign that *Anomoepus* was made by a primitive form of ornithischian dinosaur. It was a turkey-sized plant-eater, with a small head, long tail and relatively long limbs for a small animal.

Anomoepus footprints show that it walked on two legs but at times had all four on the ground. It may have used its five-fingered hands to grab plant material. It was not unusual for traces of its tail also to be seen. It took steps less than a foot long with its feet spread almost as wide, suggesting a plant-eater.

Stone slabs from the Hitchcock Collection suggest *Anomoepus* trackmakers were gregarious and congregated in groups, as some later ornithischian dinosaurs are known to have done. Footprints of several individuals of different sizes are not unusual. Some are small enough that Paul thinks they suggest the presence of juvenile dinosaurs being cared for by adults.

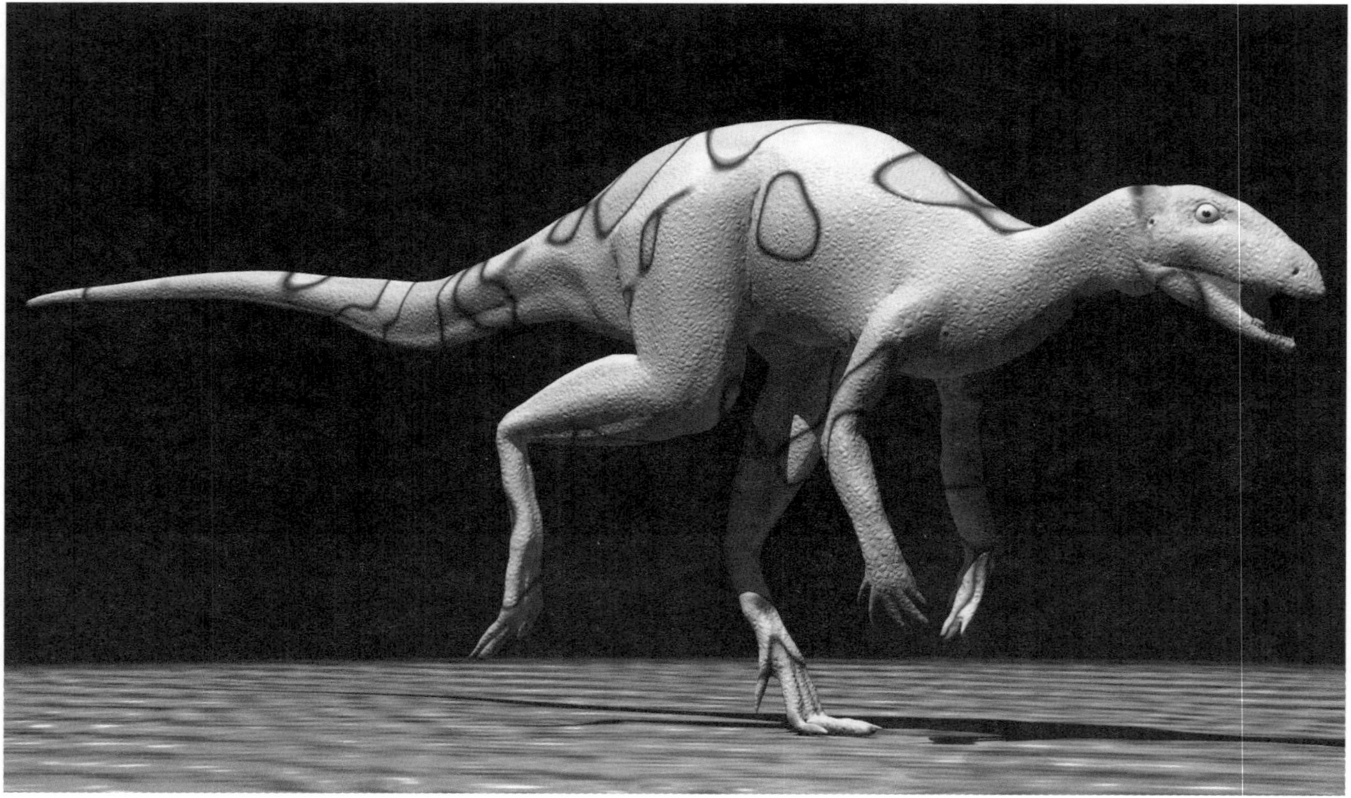

An early form of ornithischian dinosaur similar to *Lesothosaurus*, by Will Sillin.

Possible *Anomoepus* Trackmaker

Lesothosaurus diagnosticus
"Lesotho lizard"
Ornithischian dinosaur
Skulls & partial skeleton
Early Jurassic
Discovered: Lesotho, Africa
1963

Dinosaur State Park 9

A meat-eating dinosaur searches a Connecticut Valley lakeshore like one that existed at Dinosaur State Park in the ancient past.

Beneath the dome at Dinosaur State Park is a large trackway marked with hundreds of dinosaur footprints. Exhibits include fossils, dioramas, dinosaur reconstructions and murals depicting life in the Connecticut Valley early in the age of dinosaurs. Outside, there is a casting area where visitors can make plaster casts of *Eubrontes* footprints, the marks of a large, meat-eating dinosaur. There is also an arboretum featuring plants and coniferous trees like those that existed during Mesozoic time.

How to get there: From the north, take I-91 to Exit 23 and turn right (east) on West Street. From the south, take Exit 23 and turn left (east) on West Street. The entrance to Dinosaur State Park is less than a mile down the road on the right (south) side. The park is open Tuesdays through Sundays. There is a fee for admission to the trackway and exhibits. Parking is free.

Introduction

Terrestrial dinosaurs may be long gone, but there are still a few places where it's possible to imagine what the world was like when the great beasts first came to dominate life on earth. There is no better place to do it than the strip of Mesozoic lakeshore preserved at the Dinosaur State Park in Rocky Hill, Connecticut.

Dinosaur State Park is unlike other dinosaur museums. It doesn't display dinosaur skeletons strung together with iron pipes the way people are accustomed to seeing them. It shows a different side of dinosaurs altogether. "You see a skeleton in the museum and that's one thing. Of course, it doesn't have any flesh on it," Peter Galton says. "But when you see footprints in places where dinosaurs actually walked, and you compare them with your own diminutive feet, it's something else."

Dinosaur State Park preserves a brief slice of time, perhaps as short as a day or as long as weeks, in the life of a dinosaur community. It is where dinosaurs came to eat and drink some 200 million years ago. Most of the footprints in the park remain much as they were when the last dinosaur passed along this bit of lakeshore long ago.

All it takes is a bit of imagination to travel back to that time. Go to the park on a hot, summer day and the air might hang as it did on humid days when dinosaurs lived in the Connecticut Valley. Stroll around the arboretum and be surrounded by plants much like the plants that lived then. Enter the dome and go face-to-face with life-size recreations of the meat-eating theropod dinosaurs that came here in large numbers. Look down at the trackway and see the many hundreds of footprints they left as they trotted along the lakeshore in search of a meal—many looking as if they were made yesterday.

Dinosaur State Park and the science of paleontology

Dinosaur State Park is different from other museums in another significant respect. While as many as 80,000 tourists visit

The dome covering the trackway and exhibits at Dinosaur State Park.

the park each year, paleontologists from around the world also make frequent visits. The park is much more than a museum; it is also a rare, natural laboratory used for scientific research.

Paul Olsen comes here to study fossils and discuss the nature of the park with colleagues. He has gathered a great deal of evidence suggesting that Dinosaur State Park is one of the rare places in the world to glimpse what dinosaurs were like very early in their history, some 200 million years ago.

Dinosaur State Park has helped Paul develop his theory for how dinosaurs, once just a few relatively small reptiles, grew to become the great giants that captured the popular imagination. He believes the footprints here are evidence that dinosaurs inherited the earth only after surviving a global mass extinction at the boundary between Triassic and Jurassic time. The catastrophe gave dinosaurs a chance to expand, and to grow to dominate life on earth for 135 million years.

The world a "day after" extinction

Footprints found at the park, and at other locations in the Connecticut Valley, show the effect Paul believes the extinction had on life on earth. They reveal how there were fewer kinds of animals after the Triassic-Jurassic boundary than existed before. Many forms of animals, especially early reptiles, had disappeared.

Survivors included dinosaurs, crocodiles and early mammals. The first large, meat-eating, theropod dinosaurs appeared almost immediately following the extinction and early dinosaurs rapidly expanded into Early Jurassic environments—just like the one preserved at the park.

"The wonderful thing about Dinosaur State Park," says Paul, "is that the footprints represent an assemblage of dinosaurs that lived only about 600,000 years after the Triassic-Jurassic boundary. They're the survivors of that mass extinction. You're looking at a dinosaur community that would evolve into the great dinosaurian communities of the Late Jurassic."

But the recovery of life on earth was still a long way off. "It took 20 million years to recover levels of diversity that existed in the Triassic," Paul emphasizes. He wonders if what has been learned of the Triassic-Jurassic extinction at places like Dinosaur State Park may not be important to the future of our own species. "We're seeing similar changes in our own time," Paul says, referring to high rates of extinction today, "and the world won't be the same after. For life to get back to where it is now could take another 20 million years."

The environment early in the age of dinosaurs

The Connecticut Valley at the beginning of the Jurassic Period was littered with lakes and ponds. Aquatic communities of fish and plants thrived in the shallows, and terrestrial animals, including dinosaurs, inhabited the mudflats and lakeshores. Dinosaur State Park preserves a portion of one of these communities from the past.

"What you're seeing at Dinosaur State Park is the shoreline

of a lake, and in that particular case a lake which is drying up and drying up fast," Paul explains. "It was a huge lake, covering tens of thousands of square miles, and it's evaporating. How fast? On a scale of thousands of years.

"You're looking at a shoreline of that lake as it's receding. Dinosaurs were following that shoreline out, following the food source, following the water, and those are a few of the reasons they were there."

Lake levels rose and fell following climatic cycles. "The same climate changes which we see as responsible for that are still functioning today," Paul says. The climate of the Connecticut Valley in the Early Jurassic cycled back and forth between dry seasons and wet seasons and the lakes dried out and filled up according to these cycles. The cycles were in turn influenced by the gravitational pulls of other planets of the solar system, a pattern that continues into the present.

An upside-down community

The communities of animals that lived along Connecticut Valley lakeshores were not only less diverse following the extinction at the Triassic-Jurassic boundary, they were "upside down" compared to natural communities today. "It was a very strange ecosystem," Paul observes, "where carnivores were more common than herbivores." That fact becomes apparent from the moment you look at the tracks under the dome. All are of a large, meat-eating, theropod dinosaur known from the footprint *Eubrontes*.

The classic food chain pyramid, usually drawn with many plant-eaters at its base, and a few meat-eaters at its peak, seems flipped upside down. The evidence suggests that there were relatively few herbivores and a great many carnivores—just the opposite of what would normally be expected.

"That would be true if the carnivores are eating the herbivores," Paul argues, "but if you have a world in which herbivores are not very common, you can still have a lot of carnivores who are feeding on smaller carnivores or aquatic animals." The carnivores, including animals that made the footprints *Eubrontes* and *Grallator*, were likely not very picky eaters, but instead snapped at just about anything that moved.

"Ecological release" & the expansion of the dinosaurs

Paul believes the riddle of the upside-down community, and in a broader sense the expansion of the dinosaurs that began here, can be explained by the concept of ecological release theorized by the renowned biologist, E. O. Wilson. The idea is that theropod dinosaurs that survived the Triassic-Jurassic extinction arrived in a world where they no longer had any large, nondinosaurian meat-eaters to compete with for prey. They were new "kings of the hill" and could go after pretty much whatever caught their attention.

"Basically, competitors have been wiped out," Paul proposes. "I'll give you a good example. If you went to the average lakeshore at the end of the Triassic, the top carnivore you would see would be a phytosaur—a long-snouted, carnivorous, distant relative of crocodiles. You'd see them, and then you'd get out of the way because some were very, very large."

"If you were to go inland a bit," Paul continues, "you'd see another carnivore, probably the top carnivore called a rauisuchian [such as *Postosuchus*], also a distant crocodile relative. They could get very, very large, with skulls as big as *Tyrannosaurus rex*. They're not very well known, but they were very common in the Triassic, and you'd want to get away from them, too.

"Well, you get into the earliest Jurassic [which is where you are at Dinosaur State Park] after this mass extinction and those guys are not around," Paul explains. "What seems to immediately happen is that carnivorous dinosaurs start taking over that semiaquatic niche. They're not swimming in the water, but they're living like shorebirds, like cranes or herons, eating fish and running after small crocodilians, as well as the first few herbivores that are around.

"So, they're sort of all-purpose carnivores," Paul concludes.

The model of Dilophosaurus, a theropod that may have been like the dinosaurs that made the Eubrontes footprints seen in the trackway.

"It's not a quirk that herbivores are rare. You see this generalization—all-purpose carnivores. What you see is what you're getting. You're seeing something that was characteristic of that period. It wasn't characteristic of the period before and it wasn't characteristic 20 million years after. This is something inherent to that period—and not just in the Connecticut Valley. This was a global phenomenon."

The presence of large numbers of large theropods is easy to see. *Eubrontes* footprints dominate at Dinosaur State Park. No evidence of any plant-eating dinosaurs at all is exposed at the site. And it's not just in the valley that upside-down, theropod-dominated track sites are found after the Triassic-Jurassic boundary. Paul's claim that it was a global phenomenon is supported by what Martin Lockley has found in the western United States as well.

"Ninety percent of sites in the western United States in the Early Jurassic are also dominated by theropods," agrees Martin, "and there are certainly sites with multiple theropod trackways. I was mapping a site recently where there were just tons of these things going in all different directions."

Spencer Lucas has an opposing view. Spencer disputes the ideas that Dinosaur State Park gives evidence of an upside-down community and that larger theropods like the Connecticut Valley trackmakers appeared first in the Early Jurassic. "Large theropods were around in the Late Triassic," Spencer counters, pointing to evidence from Australia, Germany and New Mexico, "which disproves ideas about ecological release at the beginning of the Jurassic."

The layout

To discover the world early in the age of dinosaurs, start your trip by walking along the geologic column, or the timescale for the ages of the earth, in the paved walkway leading from the parking lot. A 92-foot section of the walkway depicts the major milestones in the history of life on earth. Much of the base of the column is conspicuously empty, an indication of how little is actually known of the earth's 4.6 billion-year history.

Dinosaurs lived in the Mesozoic Era, well up the column, represented by a gray stone panel. "Clearly, dinosaurs did not live 'when the earth was young' as many people believe," says Greg McHone, "but they lived comparatively recently judged against the age of the earth.

Our own time, the Cenozoic Era, or the "Age of Mammals," makes up just the last 16 inches of geological time. Human history takes up less space than the line in the pavement separating the last panel, above the word "MAN."

From the geographic column follow the red silhouetted footprints toward the dome. These silhouettes represent the footprints of *Eubrontes*, the Connecticut State Fossil, made by a famous meat-eating dinosaur that once hunted here.

The walkway leads through part of the "Arboretum of

Evolution," created by geologist and former park supervisor Rich Krueger over several decades. The arboretum extends around the dome and out to West Street. Ahead and across the lawn, just before the walk turns to the right, is the first tree planted, an ancient form of tree known as a Dawn Redwood. Behind is the entrance to the park's walking trails.

One of the most fun and memorable areas of the park, the footprint casting area, is on the left, approaching the dome. Inside the dome are the ticket counter, a gift shop, the exhibits and the footprint trackway. A second, larger footprint trackway remains buried on the parking lot side of the dome.

The trackway

Enter the dome to get your tickets and make your way through the gift shop to the trackway and exhibit areas. Ahead is an excellent place to get a first look at the trackway. The trackway is made up of an outcrop of sandstone layers that preserves as many as 500 footprints. Most occur on two relatively thin layers of sediment. The sandstone trackway tilts slightly in the general

The trackway exposed beneath the dome at Dinosaur State Park

direction of the valley's eastern border fault.

Conditions that existed in the Connecticut Valley early in the dinosaur age helped to make the valley a perfect place for preserving footprints and other trace fossils. The rise and fall of the local lakes left muddy shores that at times had just the right consistency, not too wet and not too dry, for impressions of everything from tube worms to dinosaurs to be preserved and later naturally cemented into stone.

All of the footprints on the trackway under the dome at Dinosaur State Park are the *Eubrontes* type. (There are a few *Grallator* footprints on the large, buried trackway to the east of the building.) The *Eubrontes* footprints may have been made by a theropod dinosaur similar to *Dilophosaurus*, depicted by the model and the mural on the opposite side of the trackway. Peter Galton and Jim Farlow have reported that the footprints measure about 12 to 16 inches from heel to toe. The theropods that made them were walking at a relatively slow pace, taking steps about four feet long, and moving relatively slowly at perhaps five to seven miles per hour.

There is no evidence to suggest the animals were moving as a herd or followed a physical path such as the shoreline. Rather, the tracks seem to suggest a succession of individual dinosaurs coming to prowl the lakeshore, periodically shifting direction as they searched randomly for things to eat over a period of days or weeks. Paleontologist John Ostrom speculated that the footprints at Dinosaur State Park were made in as short a time as 24 hours, or just long enough for a dinosaur to leave its prints along a lakeshore and for them to be covered over by mud and silt.

"That's possible, but I don't think it's true," disagrees Paul. "When you have a shoreline like that the mud often gets coated with a slime of bacteria and algae that holds the moisture for much longer than it would remain otherwise. As a result, the track surface probably remains suitable for quite a long time. I've seen that happen. It has two consequences. One is that the animals' feet don't stick to the mud when they walk over it, and the other is that the mud doesn't dry out for a really long period of time."

When conditions are right and a track is quickly buried, it may be hardened by natural chemical processes of cementation that work to turn mud or silt into sandstone, like the layers of rock preserved at the park.

"I think the limiting factor was how fast the mud dried," Rick Krueger concludes. "In a subtropical climate, a one-inch layer of mud would dry rapidly and then cracks would appear. The absence of cracks on this surface suggests burial took place quickly—within a week, algae notwithstanding."

The magic of mica

"Mica is a mineral found in the metamorphic rocks of the eastern highlands that were a source of the Connecticut Valley sediments," Rich Krueger explains. "When the bedding plane at the park was first uncovered it glistened with mica flakes. The flakes acted like teflon, so the mud didn't stick to animals' feet, and during excavation it acted as a release. Without mica, the tracks would never have been found because the layers of rock wouldn't have split open. This was why I stressed aspects of the "geological setting" in the park's exhibits as well as the valley's paleontology; the two are inseparable.

The mystery of the swimmer tracks

Most of the tracks in the park are well known, but a mystery surrounds the so-called "swimmer tracks" seen through the fixed telescope in the first viewing area. In 1980, Massachusetts-based Walter Coombs suggested these smaller impressions were the marks of dinosaurs swimming, moving along the surface of the lake and reaching down to push along the bottom with their toes.

"Unfortunately, I don't think he's correct," counters Peter Galton. He points to a study done by Australian ichnologists Thulborn and Wade that suggests the marks were the result of a

179

dinosaur walking over a lakeshore which had dried enough in places to prevent all but the beast's toes from breaking through its crusty surface.

"The other problem, of course, is a hydraulic problem," Peter says. "To get these swimming tracks the water would have to be as high as a dinosaur's hips and then go down to leave a mudflat on which all the other tracks can be made. However you look at it, that's a lot of water. It would take months to disappear. It seems unlikely the swimming tracks would remain well preserved for that long."

The history of the park

The first group of exhibits at the park tells the remarkable story of the site's discovery by bulldozer operator Edward McCarthy and its subsequent preservation. McCarthy not only made the most important discovery of fossil footprints by an amateur in the valley since Pliny Moody uncovered *Noah's Raven*, but his quick thinking led to Dinosaur State Park becoming the place it is today. He left the people of Connecticut a great legacy.

Late in the summer of 1966, McCarthy was busy digging a foundation for a new State Highway Department Building when he uncovered six footprints buried about twelve feet underground. He climbed down off the bulldozer he was operating and reported the find to the architect and engineer supervising the work. Calls for help went out to scientists at the Peabody Museum, to local universities, and the State Geological and Natural History Survey.

Just weeks later, on September 13th, Connecticut Governor John Dempsey announced the creation of Dinosaur State Park. Careful excavation of a large area of footprints was begun under the direction of the Peabody Museum's Grant Meyer and with the help of student volunteers. By October, a large trackway of roughly 1,500 dinosaur footprints was exposed.

Sid Quarrier directed the excavation of the second, smaller trackway in 1967, revealing another 500 or so footprints. An inflatable building was put up over the smaller trackway shortly before the park officially opened in October 1968.

The inflatable building was replaced with the current dome in 1978 after several storms left the original cover in tatters on the ground, and forced the temporary closing of the park. In the summer, the large trackway was open. In the winter, it was covered with vinyl sheeting, heating cables, sand, sawdust, more vinyl sheeting, and old tires. Sump pumps were also added to lower the water table. The trackway was reburied in 1975 to prevent damage from further exposure. It remains buried beneath the lawn on the parking lot side of the dome, with concrete blocks marking its corners, waiting for a permanent building of its own.

Surveys & mapping

Several photos and maps in the first exhibit area also record the first surveys and maps Sid Quarrier and Peter Galton made of the trackways. Sid was then a geologist for the State. Peter was doing his postdoctoral research and managing the collection at the Peabody Museum.

Sid Quarrier takes photos.
Courtesy, Peter Galton

To map the large trackway, they marked off ten-foot squares with pieces of tape and then photographed each square. The pictures were then pasted up to make a photo mosaic record of the trackway. "Sid and I took photographs of the main exposure," Peter remembers. "He tied a ladder to the front bumper of his Land Rover and climbed up to make photographs. Mapping the inside area was much more

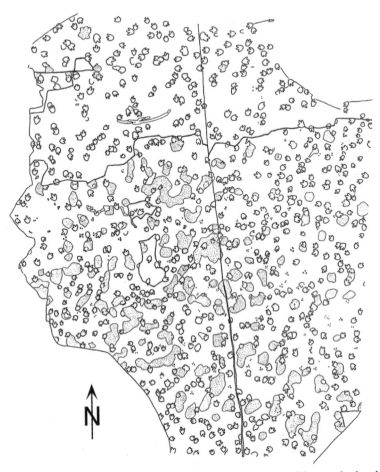

The map Peter Galton made of the trackway exposed beneath the dome.
Courtesy, Peter Galton

tricky because the dome had been put over. So, I made a wood frame five feet square with clear plastic across it. I'd lay that down, trace out the footprints, stand it up against a white background, photograph it, then wipe off the ink, put it down and do it over again for the whole area."

Hitchcock's books & "the Bones from the Well"

Beyond the exhibits of the park's history is a glass case dedicated to the history of paleontology in the Connecticut Valley. Inside are original publications of two of Edward Hitchcock's famous footprint studies, from 1841 and 1858.

There are also casts of the earliest verifiable dinosaur bones found in North America, "the Bones from the Well" discovered in East Windsor, Connecticut, in 1818. Identified as a indeterminate prosauropod dinosaur by Peter Galton in 1976, the bones were discovered more than two decades before the British scientist Richard Owen first coined the term "dinosaur" to categorize three large, extinct reptiles found in England.

Connecticut Valley dinosaur footprints

Besides the tracks in the ground, the park also has the footprints of other dinosaurs known from the valley on display. There is a slab containing *Anomoepus* footprints on loan from Nick McDonald, a local geologist and an expert on the fossils of the Connecticut Valley. The *Anomoepus* footprints are believed

Hitchcock's Supplement to the Ichnology of New England with reproductions of "the Bones from the Well."

to have been made by a small ornithischian dinosaur. McDonald's fossil at the park includes a "tail drag," an impression the animal may have left in the mud when it slowed down and its tail dragged.

Beneath a large model of the valley's "layer cake" of sedimentary rocks are specimens of the footprints *Otozoum* and *Grallator* and the reptile footprints *Batrachopus* and *Antipus*. The *Otozoum* tracks are remarkable not just for their size and shape, but also for the impressions they preserve of the skin of the underside of the animal's feet.

The footprint Otozoum

Across the room is a model of *Coelophysis*—a small theropod dinosaur known from the earlier Triassic Period. *Coelophysis* may have been similar to the small theropod dinosaur that made *Grallator*. Nearby are casts of *Coelophysis* skeletons and the tooth of a small theropod dinosaur from Connecticut.

Tracks and traces

Most of the tracks in Dinosaur State Park are impressed in two layers of sandstone. Many on the top layer also left impressions on the lower layer, a common condition which can make drawing the shape of a footprint or measuring its dimensions a complicated task.

The display describing "over tracks", "true tracks" and "under tracks" depicts how ichnologists have come to recognize characteristics of a single footprint impressed on multiple layers. The concept of true tracks has been expanded in recent years by the work of biologist Stephen Gatesy. Stephen has shown how footprints that were impressed deeply in mud may also preserve a detailed record of how dinosaurs actually walked.

Dinosaur footprints were by no means the only traces of ancient life preserved in the sediments of the Connecticut Valley. There is also abundant evidence of events as subtle as breezes across the surface of a lake, passing rain showers, and dry, cracked mud. Several examples of these kinds of trace fossils are also displayed.

The environment

Continuing through the exhibit area, and just before the far entrance to the trackway area, are a diorama and displays of fossil plants. These depict and document the plant life that typified local environments just before and immediately following the Triassic-Jurassic boundary.

"The small diorama was donated by The Friends of Dinosaur Park & Arboretum," notes Rich Krueger. The Friends of Dinosaur Park & Arboretum is a private, non-profit organization that has been dedicated to protecting and preserving the park since it was established in 1976.

"The diorama is divided into halves. On the left is the Triassic environment and on the right is the Jurassic environment. Those strange-looking things that have branched out are seed ferns. They were the progenitors of modern flowering plants. They are also the only major group of plants in the history of the earth to go extinct. There are cycads and ferns of all kinds. The ferns with the broad leaves, in the middle, were known as *Clathopteris*. Next to those you've got conifers, gingko trees, some horsetails, and mosses, including *Lycopodeum*. These are plants that are still around today.

"Our dioramas are designed to display what has been learned of Mesozoic plants by people like Bruce Cornet who studied fossil pollen found in the valley," Rich continues. "Pollen and spores are productive sources of information about plants because they don't deteriorate. The evidence for what is in this diorama can be seen in the displays just to the left of it. They are all fossils from the Connecticut Valley. Many of these, and several of the small trackways on display in the building, were collected by Nick McDonald and Bruce Cornet. Others are on loan to the park from Wesleyan University."

Much of what is known of the local climate in the Late Triassic and Early Jurassic has been learned from Bruce's studies of fossil leaves. Fossil leaf structures can sometimes reveal information about temperature, humidity and atmospheric conditions that existed while the plants were living.

Just beyond the diorama and fossil displays is the ramp across the trackway. As you proceed onto the ramp, models of a flying reptile, the pterosaur known as *Dimorphodon* hang above on the right. "There isn't any evidence of those here," says Rich, "but there is no reason that they couldn't have been here. We may never find [evidence of them in Connecticut] because conditions here didn't preserve animals like these."

Just ahead and also on the right is the park's model of a large theropod dinosaur set against a mural of a wide sweep of lake margin like that which existed here in the Early Jurassic. The lakes of the Connecticut Valley at that time were centers of terrestrial life, and supported diverse aquatic communities as well. Not only did the lakes preserve footprint and trace fossils along their shores, they also preserved the remains of fish in the layers of silt that collected on the lake bottoms.

The theropod, known as *Dilophosaurus*, is known from bones found in Arizona. It may have made a footprint like the *Eubrontes* footprints seen at the park. Measured against other Connecticut Valley dinosaurs it was a big predator, but a pup compared to theropods that came later, such as *Tyrannosaurus rex*.

"This model was assembled in 1980," says Rich. "It was the first model of *Dilophosaurus* ever made and the first major project undertaken here by The Friends of Dinosaur Park & Arboretum. We had no exhibits up until that time. The model was originally installed on a gravel floor, in an essentially empty building."

Continuing down the ramp, groups of much smaller plant-eating dinosaurs are seen foraging among primitive horsetail plants. Early dinosaurs like these models of turkey-sized ornithischians may have made the footprint *Anomoepus*. Next to them are models of the prosauropod *Anchisaurus*. This dinosaur, along with a similar species, *Ammosaurus*, is known from several skeletons found in the valley. *Anchisaurus* or *Ammosaurus* may have made the footprint *Otozoum*.

"The prosauropods took advantage of the plants," Rich says. "They started growing longer necks so they could reach up higher than the small ornithischians. They prospered and eventually grew into the giant sauropods. The little guys [the ornithischians] were the ancestors of many others, such as duck-billed dinosaurs."

Will Sillin's mural: *In the Late Triassic*

On the left side of the ramp, at the lower end of the trackway, is the most famous Dinosaur State Park mural, *In the Late Triassic*. It's said a picture is worth a thousand words; the effect of Will Sillin's work in this painting is measured in millions of years.

The mural represents much of what has been learned about life around stream and lakeshore communities of the Connecticut Valley shortly before the Triassic-Jurassic boundary. Before he could paint it, Will had to bone up on practically everything paleontologists had discovered about the valley over the past two centuries. He was fortunate to have two world-class tutors to help, Paul Olsen and Bruce Cornet.

While Paul knows about the dinosaurs of the Connecticut Valley, Bruce is the expert on local fossil plants—not that he doesn't also have an uncanny knack for finding fossil fish and animals. He specializes, however, in the study of fossils of plants' reproductive cells, including spores and pollen, and plant structures like leaves. Bruce uses fossil leaves, fossil spores and pollen grains to gain all kinds of knowledge—from details of atmospheric gases in the

"In the Late Triassic"
Copyright©2004 Friends of Dinosaur State Park and Will Sillin

ancient past to the effects the events of the Triassic-Jurassic mass extinction had on plants such as ferns.

Together, Paul and Bruce took Will for a private tour of their valley. They told him what he needed to know about local geology, about how the mountainous highlands were first pushed up, and the valley settled down. They described communities of plants living in the foothills and around the lakes. They showed him fossil plants from tree ferns to cycads, and the footprints of tetrapods from reptiles to amphibians, phytosaurs and dinosaurs. After they were through, they left Will to paint it all. The result was the magnificent mural visitors see today.

A portrait of the valley in the Late Triassic Period

The mountains in the background are bare. Few plants were able to take hold on the steep slopes long enough to endure. The highlands were eroding too swiftly. Flash floods, rain and wind ground the mountains into sand and gravel and spread the tailings across the valley floor at an astonishing rate.

Forests stretched from the valley into the foothills. They were dominated by early seed plants. Among the most common were *cheirolepidaceous* conifers—evergreen trees that produced cones and needle-like leaves. They varied in size from shrubs to large trees.

Nearer the lakes the forests grew more diverse. The forest floor was covered with cycads, horsetail rushes, tree ferns and ferns. The cycles of their growth and decay supported a variety of insects and invertebrates. Plant material collected on the ground and was converted to compost by insects, worms and bacteria. Streams and rains carried nutrients across the mudflats and into the lakes.

Depicted in the mural are a few reptiles that would survive the Triassic-Jurassic extinction, including a small theropod dinosaur similar to *Coelophysis*. Also shown is an early form of crocodile similar to *Protosuchus* and the prosauropod dinosaur *Anchisaurus*.

Below the mural, arranged in the diorama in front, are the fallen. Here are models of several tetrapods that disappeared in the Late Triassic—a phytosaur *Rutiodon*, the amphibian *Metoposaurus* and the primitive, procolophonid reptile, *Hysognathus*—several made with the assistance of paleontologist Donald Baird.

Species flocks

Among the fish in Connecticut Valley lakes in the Early Jurassic were species called semionotids. Semionotids had the capability to evolve rapidly relative to other sorts of animals, probably in response to changes in the habitats that existed around the shoreline. Many species of semionotids appeared and later went extinct.

The fish were examples of what evolutionary biologists have come to know as "species flocks." Biologist P. Humphrey Greenwood proposed the concept in the 1970s to describe closely related species that develop and live together in the same ecosystem. Examples are found today in places like Lake Malawi, Africa, where ichthyologists (biologists who study fish) continue to explore the evolutionary implications of species flocks by studying populations of fish known as cichlids.

Looking at the past, it appears that some living things may have had the ability to change or evolve more rapidly than others. These life forms led relatively quickly to the appearance of many

new, closely related species.
All had certain characteristics
in common that were unique
to their groups. It's thought
that the many flocks of
semionotid species in local
lakes each evolved from single
ancestors and in response to
environmental conditions in the
valley and the lakes early in the
age of dinosaurs.

Rich Krueger
Photo: Peter Galton

The arboretum

It wasn't long after the
decision was made to preserve
the trackways at Rocky Hill
that a new question came up.
What sort of park should it be?
"No one knew what to do with
it," says Rich Krueger, who signed on as the park's first supervisor
in 1970. "There had not been any preservation of any track site
anywhere in the country before."

Many different groups pitched in with ideas, including a
committee of local teachers. "One of the ideas they came up with
was not to landscape the grounds in the typical way, but to plant
it with plants that lived in the age of dinosaurs," says Rich. "They
didn't give any further direction than that; it was just a gleam of an
idea. I was really excited about that possibility, and that was one of
the reasons I took the job."

Just the gleam of an idea was enough for Rich to imagine how
the park might come to look—and that was very different from the
way it was in the beginning. There was only a temporary building
at first, and it came down in a snowstorm. "When I arrived, the
building was in terrible shape. It had collapsed during the winter.

It was flat on the ground when I first saw it. The grounds were just a construction site. There were piles of debris all over the place. There was no picnic area. There was just one table. There was nothing."

There would be nothing for seven more years, while plans were sorted out. In the meantime, Rich cut nature trails and started reading everything he could about plants from the age of dinosaurs. "I started collecting files; I'm a pack rat when it comes to literature. Everywhere I went, I'd collect stuff on paleobotany [the study of plants from fossils] and make notes about what I thought would grow here. I've just kept adding to that. Today, we have hundreds of articles and books."

Rich started planting trees in 1978. "The Connecticut Tree Protection Association donated 20 Dawn Redwood trees to the park and the state allowed them to be planted," Rich says. "We had a little ceremony and planted them around the grounds." Dawn Redwoods are believed to be as much as 100 million years old.

More donations followed. Ted Childs, the owner of the state's largest private forest in Norfolk, donated twenty more trees. People sent small donations of money and a horticultural fund was started. The Friends of Dinosaur Park & Arboretum raised more money. It wasn't much, but enough to keep Rich going.

"I started buying small plants, I mean this big," Rich says, holding his thumb and index finger a couple of inches apart. "I started buying rooted cuttings through mail order, and I started planting them around." He didn't have money to buy large trees, but he could afford small cuttings. They would grow big soon enough.

In 1985, the state set aside funds for more landscaping and Rich had planters built outside the dome that replaced the temporary building. He's been filling in the grounds ever since. "I set up a nursery in my backyard," Rich recalls. "We didn't have a water supply [in a corner of the park he'd been using as a nursery]

and we couldn't handle the weeds and everything else. I could do it much better at home, where I could control the situation."

Rich's yard filled with buckets that made it easier to grow trees from small cuttings. "I started containerizing plants and growing them to a larger size before putting them out. Early on, people would pull them out of the ground or step on them—they were too little. I finally developed a system and grew hundreds and hundreds of plants at a really low cost—most were under five dollars."

From a few cuttings: An arboretum

Rich's cuttings have since grown and survived many harsh Connecticut winters. More than 400 species of plants now fill the park, including 200 species of conifers. The results are amazing; the American Conifer Society now lists the Dinosaur State Park Arboretum among the top conifer gardens in the country—but conifers aren't the only special aspect of the grounds.

"We grow plants whose ancestors lived in the Mesozoic Era," Rich explains. "The general effect is conifers with primitive, flowering plants stuck in between. Conifers form the backbone of the garden and everything else is around them."

"As far as the arrangement on the grounds goes, it looks like it doesn't make any sense, but it does. I started grouping plants according to exposure and soils. For example, the firs need deep, rich, cool soils, and they're in the best soil on the whole property. It's a north-facing slope, so that's where I put the firs and they've done very well. Spruces can take a little more heat; I put them over where the soils were poorer and flatter. The pines—they can take anything, so I put them on the worst compacted, most miserable piles of soil that we have. Junipers can take even poorer conditions, so they're

planted on a rock outcrop in a rock garden.

"Secondarily," Rich continues "I also grew a couple of groupings of plants according to their origin—where they came from. I have a collection of southeastern plants, including bald cypress and black gum and sycamore. They're all ancient. They all go back to the Cretaceous. I have a small collection of European plants. A tiny collection of western conifers and a collection of plants from Japan and China are all in one area. So I have segregated them a bit that way.

"In the front of the building it's a mish-mash of everything," Rich acknowledges. "These conifers are mostly dwarf plants and they were laid out more for aesthetic reasons, to look attractive. That's the way I grouped them, so they would be slow growing and just to look nice. Mainly what we have here in front of the building are *Cryptomerias* and *Chamaecyparis* from Asia, along with some dwarf pines and dwarf yews and some junipers.

"We have gymnosperms [the "naked seed" plants, including conifers, that dominated much of the dinosaur age] and gingkos as the old, old plants. Gingkos [the living fossil plant] are the oldest plants we have in the park. Among other examples of ancient trees is an *Araucaria*, or Monkey Puzzle Tree.

"The angiosperms are divided into two groups, the monocots and the dicots. The dicots are later; they include grasses, bamboos, palm trees, lily family, that kind of thing. Those things don't fit at all into this scenario, so we're dealing with the early dicots and that includes plants like the *Katsura* trees and magnolias near the main entrance.

"Now, we've got a couple of exceptions to that rule," Rich says. "One, we're growing any conifer at all that will live in this area. We go by family, that is, trees in families that existed in the Mesozoic. For example, a spruce tree didn't live at the time of the dinosaurs, but it's in the pine family. The pine family was in existence at the time of the dinosaurs. It evolved to add several branches—larches,

193

for example, are another modern group of members of the pine family. They didn't exist back then, but these are modern versions of plants that did and later went extinct.

"Another exception is that I've put in a few flowering plants, known as angiosperms, like dogwoods, that are right on the borderline between the Mesozoic and the Tertiary," says Rich. "It may turn out that someday they'll find evidence of these particular angiosperms in the Mesozoic; they're pretty close. A lot of plants evolved at the end of the Mesozoic and the beginning of the Tertiary and new discoveries are still being made.

"And then I put in a few plants just for effect; for example I've grown bamboo in our Asian garden. Bamboo wasn't around then. So, I put it in to make it look like an Asian garden. A few things like that, but otherwise it's pretty much, as far as I can figure, what was around in the Mesozoic."

The best is yet to come

"A landscape like this is never static," Rich explains. He should know. Even in retirement, keeping the arboretum healthy requires a great deal of his time. It's the changes still to come that he is most eager to see. "The real value of this garden will grow with age. An old garden is a treasure and this garden is still very, very young. A lot of these plants are less than ten or fifteen years old." Thanks to Rich they will grow to be magnificent. "There's a long way to go," he comments, distracted by something he sees that needs pruning. "This is my baby and I'll keep it going."

The casting area

Perhaps one of the greatest features of the park is that anyone who wants to can go home with a dinosaur footprint—a plaster cast of a footprint that is. Several *Eubrontes* footprints are set out in the casting area and are available for visitors to use to make casts of their own.

The park provides casting rings and water. Visitors have to bring their own cooking oil, rags, paper towels, five-gallon plastic bucket and ten pounds of plaster of paris. The entire process takes only about 30 to 45 minutes.

Making a dinosaur footprint, step-by-step:

1. Clean the track and metal ring with broom. ***Do not use water!***
2. Oil the track and the metal ring with your hands.
3. Center ring on the track and wrap rags outside of the ring.
4. Pour three quarts of water (3/4 gallon) into the bucket.
5. Add ten pounds of plaster of paris.
6. Stir the plaster until it is smooth and thick, preferably by hand.
7. Immediately pour the mixture into the prepared ring.
8. After the cast is hard, remove the rags and the ring.
9. Remove the cast from the rock and clean off the track and ring.

Casts may be made from May 1 to October 31, from 9 a.m. to 3:30 p.m. The process does not work well in wet weather and the area is closed in winter.

Powder Hill Dinosaur Park, Middlefield

A small brownstone quarry has been turned into a little-known Middlefield town park where you can see several large and small dinosaur footprints. In addition to the tracks, you can see good examples of East Berlin siltstone, which seems to be the formation with the most footprints.

How to get there: Take Route 66 east from Meriden or west from Middletown to Route 147, and turn south onto that road toward the Powder Ridge Ski Area. In Baileyville (a tiny mill village), turn right onto Powder Hill Road and continue about one mile past the entrance to the ski area. The park is on your right.

The layers of fine-grained sandstone or siltstone at the park are "parted" along bedding planes, probably due to clay that washes out more easily between the layers. The parting also made it easier for the quarry workers to split out blocks of similar thickness and size, which would make them more valuable as building stones.

These sediments probably were deposited in a lake, which had a bottom of fine sand of uniform size, along with some mud and clay. If the water was shallow or the mud was sometimes exposed due to low water levels, animals would leave tracks. In order for the tracks to be preserved, the mud must have become somewhat dried and hardened, but it was soon covered by more mud when the lake level rose again.

Several different dinosaur track genera have been found at this site, such as *Eubrontes*, *Grallator* and *Anomoepus*. The first two are three-toed, theropod tracks that differ in size from large to small, which might represent either different animal species or the same species at different ages.

The Yale Peabody Museum 10

The Great Hall of the Peabody Museum displays a collection of dinosaur skeletons, including many all-time favorites such as *Apatosaurus*, *Stegosaurus* and *Triceratops*. Also on display are fossil fish, toothed birds, a giant turtle, plants, petrified wood and more. Rudolph Zallinger's famous mural *The Age of Reptiles*, the painting that spans over 300 million years of natural history, crowns a room filled with many of paleontology's gems.

How to get there: Traveling north or south on I-91, take Exit 3 off I-91 in New Haven. Continue on to the Trumbull Street Connector. At the second intersection, turn right onto Whitney Avenue. The Peabody Museum is located at 170 Whitney Avenue on the corner of Whitney Avenue and Sachem Street. Limited parking is available just north of the museum.

The museum is open Monday through Saturday from 10 a.m. to 5 p.m. and on Sunday from noon to 5 p.m. The best times to visit are afternoons and weekends. Admission is charged.

Introduction

A large portion of the fossil vertebrate collection of the Peabody Museum was built under the direction of Othniel Charles Marsh. He led Yale students on four fossil-hunting expeditions in the 1870s and kept crews of full-time workers busy year-round excavating several of the now famous bone sites in the American West from the late 1870s to the early 1890s. So many dinosaur bones were recovered by Marsh and other famous bone hunters (including Edward Drinker Cope and Barnum Brown) during that time, that the era has become known as the great dinosaur "bone rush."

Hundreds of crates of bones were shipped to New Haven by rail, where many are now on display in the Peabody's Great Hall of Dinosaurs. The Yale Peabody Museum Collection, which already included the bones of the dinosaur found in East Windsor, Connecticut, in 1818, grew to be legendary when Marsh gave his immense collection to the museum in 1898.

The museum continues to play essential roles today in conducting dinosaur science, in teaching Yale students, and in public education. In addition to the Great Hall of Dinosaurs, the Peabody has many other halls dedicated to anthropology, geology and natural history.

The Hall of Native American Cultures displays a collection of objects from the cultures of the native peoples of North America.

Daily Life in Ancient Egypt displays an Egyptian tomb and ancient artifacts. The Hall of Mammalian Evolution includes a variety of fossils of Pleistocene mammals. The Mineral Hall includes displays of local geology and minerals. The Hall of Connecticut Birds includes specimens of local birds, as well as rare and extinct birds.

The Great Hall

The dinosaurs of the Connecticut Valley were the forerunners of many fantastic giants that followed—and the Great Hall of Dinosaurs is an excellent place to see how dinosaurs changed over time.

To reach the Great Hall, continue through the entry past the admissions desk and turn right. As you enter, it's hard not to be overwhelmed by the sight of the enormous skeletons that dominate the room the way their owners once dominated life on earth.

In addition to his passion for collecting, O. C. Marsh was interested in reconstructing dinosaur skeletons on paper. He had detailed drawings made. These drawings served later, after Marsh's death, as a basis for several of the mounted skeletons seen in the Great Hall today. Marsh's drawing of *Brontosaurus* (known today as *Apatosaurus*), based on a skeleton his crews excavated in Wyoming, and a later drawing of *Anchisaurus*, based on bones cut from a brownstone quarry near Manchester, Connecticut, were among the first reconstructions done of dinosaur skeletons.

Put next to one another, Marsh's drawings of *Anchisaurus* and *Apatosaurus* frame an incredible period in the evolution of life on earth, a time when nature, in its infinite variation, began to experiment with big bodies, and land-dwellers grew to be enormous.

Prosauropods & Sauropods

Entering the Great Hall, the huge skeleton that dominates the room is that of *Apatosaurus*. This enormous plant-eater is a saurischian dinosaur, one of the two major groups or orders which English paleontologist Harry Seely used when he created a system for classifying dinosaurs in 1888.

Compare the huge specimen of *Apatosaurus* with an earlier form of plant-eater, *Plateosaurus,* shown feeding near the center of *The Age of Reptiles* mural on the wall above the display cases and to the right of *Apatosaurus. Plateosaurus* was a Triassic, plant-eating, prosauropod dinosaur, similar in many ways to the Connecticut Valley dinosaurs *Anchisaurus* and *Ammosaurus. Plateosaurus* serves as a reasonable stand-in for *Anchisaurus* and *Ammosaurus* when comparing changes that occurred from early prosauropods, like those of the Connecticut Valley in the Early Jurassic, to the sauropod dinosaurs that came later, such as *Apatosaurus,* which appeared in the Late Jurassic.

Both *Plateosaurus* and *Anchisaurus* appeared early in the age of dinosaurs. *Plateosaurus* is known from the Late Triassic and *Anchisaurus* from the Early Jurassic. Both are distinguished by the ways they were adapted to eating plants. They had long necks for reaching plants that grew higher up, and large bellies to digest a tough, conifer needle cud. Their teeth were relatively primitive, suited more to cutting than grinding. They could walk on all fours or could rear up on their two hind legs, perhaps bracing themselves with their tails, to reach new growth and leaves beyond the reach of other smaller plant-eaters.

Apatosaurus, by comparison, was the ultimate plant-eater and one of nature's truly great

Plateosaurus

The Age of Reptiles, a mural by Rudolph F. Zallinger, Copyright©1966, 1975, 1985, 1989, Peabody Museum of Natural History, Yale University, New Haven, CT

harvesting machines. Over 70 feet long and many times taller than a man, *Apatosaurus* appeared long after *Plateosaurus* and the Connecticut Valley plant-eaters. By the Late Jurassic, saurischians like *Apatosaurus* grew many times larger than early prosauropod dinosaurs, but maintained a body style similar to those first seen in *Plateosaurus* and *Anchisaurus*.

Apatosaurus also had a long neck and capacious belly, and it walked on all fours. One notable improvement was that its teeth had evolved to become better suited to grinding tough plant fibers and processing large amounts of vegetation. In general, *Apatosaurus* is an example of how herbivorous dinosaurs like those known from the Connecticut Valley changed over 50 million years of evolution.

The Age of Reptiles mural

The magnificent mural above the display cases opposite *Apatosaurus* made the Great Hall into the Sistine Chapel of paleontology. The mural is painted on plaster applied directly to the museum wall, using a classical, fresco technique similar to the technique the Italian Renaissance artist Michelangelo employed to paint his masterpieces on the ceiling of the world's most famous chapel in Rome, Italy.

The Age of Reptiles mural was painted by artist Rudolph Zallinger and took over four and a half years to complete, including a year of preparatory studies with the Yale paleontologists. The museum remained open during its painting and visitors were able to watch his progress during the time Zallinger was at work on it. The mural, completed in 1947, received a Pulitzer Award for Painting in 1949.

The idea of the mural was to paint a picture of what was known of the history of life on earth over a period of more than 300 million years. It depicts the evolution of reptiles from the Devonian Period of more than 400 million years ago through to the end of the age of dinosaurs, some 65 million years ago.

The geologic ages, and the animal and plant life associated

The Age of Reptiles, a mural by Rudolph F. Zallinger,
Copyright©1966, 1975, 1985, 1989, Peabody Museum of Natural History,
Yale University, New Haven, CT

with each, are identified along the timescale just beneath the mural. More has been learned about the ancient past since the mural was completed in 1947, but it remains a fascinating and compelling portrait of evolution.

From right to left, the mural depicts how the first tetrapods (four-legged animals) appeared in the Devonian, having evolved from fish that crawled out of the water and onto the land. Early amphibians such as *Eryops* were followed in the Carboniferous by amniotes, animals that no longer depended on returning to the water to reproduce.

Primitive synapsids, represented by finbacks *Dimetrodon* and *Ephadosaurus*, appeared and came to dominate the land during Permian time. By the Jurassic Period, the primitive synapsids led to more advanced synapsids, including early mammals. It was early in the Permian that the world's continents came together to form the great super-continent of Pangaea. Life came to a screeching halt at the end of the period with an extinction that wiped out more than 90 percent of life on earth.

Life began its recovery in the Early Triassic. Reptiles known as archosaurs replaced primitive synapsids and eventually gave rise to early dinosaurs, including *Plateosaurus*. By the Late Triassic, Pangaea had begun to pull apart in a process known as continental rifting to form the Connecticut Valley and places like it encircling the newly formed Atlantic Ocean.

The Jurassic Period followed another extinction at the end of Triassic time. Early dinosaurs similar to *Coelophysis* and *Podokesaurus*, the surprisingly small theropod dinosaur seen in the mural, survived and began their great expansion. *Archaeopteryx*, the earliest known bird, appeared in the Late Jurassic. New forms of dinosaurs also appeared in the Late Jurassic, such as *Apatosaurus, Comptosaurus* and *Stegosaurus.* They were followed in the Cretaceous by some of the best known and most exotic of dinosaurs, including duck-billed and armored dinosaurs, as well as *Tyrannosaurus* and *Triceratops*, at the very end of the Cretaceous. Dinosaurs met a sudden end with an extinction caused by an asteroid that struck the earth 65 million years ago. After 165 million years, the age of dinosaurs came to a close, and the age of mammals began.

The valley's dinosaurs

Following along below the mural, not far beyond the Triassic-Jurassic boundary appropriately enough, is a glass case displaying replicas of some of the Connecticut Valley specimens. To the right of the case is a cast of the skeleton of *Podokesaurus*, a small theropod dinosaur discovered in a glacially transported boulder near Mount Holyoke College in South Hadley, Massachusetts. The original specimen was destroyed in a fire, but two casts survive in the Yale collection, including this one on display.

Podokesaurus may well have been the dinosaur that made the footprint known as *Grallator* and found in the Connecticut Valley. It was similar to *Coelophysis*, another dinosaur often suggested as a possible *Grallator* trackmaker, but *Podokesaurus* may be a better fit. *Coelophysis* is known from Late Triassic time, while *Podokesaurus* is now thought to have lived in the Early Jurassic.

Just below the bones is a model of *Podokesaurus* made by Marsh's successor as curator of vertebrate paleontology at the

Lull's model of Podokesaurus
Courtesy of the Peabody Museum of Natural History, Yale University, New Haven, CT

Peabody, Richard Swann Lull. Lull had a passion for Connecticut Valley dinosaurs and for making models of them, including those seen in this display. Judged by its birdlike feet, long legs and small size, *Podokesaurus* was probably a small, agile, meat-eating predator.

The Bones from the Quarry

At the left of the case are models of the skull and body of an early plant-eating dinosaur once known as *Yaleosaurus*. These are Lull's models of the dinosaur whose bones were found in the quarry of Charles O. Wolcott in Manchester, Connecticut, in 1891. *Yaleosaurus* was an earlier name. This prosauropod dinosaur lived very early in the age of dinosaurs and has since been referred to as *Anchisaurus* by Peter Galton.

More dinosaur skeletons were recovered from the Wolcott Quarry than any other site in the Connecticut Valley. The first discovery there was the rear half of a skeleton of *Ammosaurus,* "The Bones from the Bridge," found during the quarrying of brownstone blocks for the Hop Brook Bridge in 1884 and saved by Wolcott to sell to Marsh.

It was often Lull's practice to restore dinosaurs by making models, and he became known for a style that can be seen if you look closely at his model of *Yaleosaurus*. He often made models that depicted the animal as it may have appeared in life on one side and with a cut-away view of its skeleton on the other. Peer around this model and you can see portions of its skeleton on the far side.

Lull's restoration technique is especially obvious in the mounted specimen of *Monoclonius* (sometimes called *Centrosaurus*) displayed with other Cretaceous horned dinosaurs at the far end of the Great Hall.

Hitchcock's birds & Owen's *Dinornis*

Continue along the glass cases to below the palm tree in the mural to view the skeleton of a large extinct, flightless bird known as *Dinornis*. It's an example of a kind of bird called a moa that lived in New Zealand and was identified by Richard Owen from a single, six-inch-long fragment of its leg bone. Owen's initial description based on this scant evidence left him open to some criticism, but he was proven right after a more complete skeleton of *Dinornis* turned up a few years later.

Owen became famous as the man who coined the term dinosaur to describe a group of saurian reptiles from England in 1842. But it was his description of *Dinornis* that had the greatest influence on paleontologist Edward Hitchcock, a professor at Amherst College who invented the field of ichnology and was the first to study the fossil footprints of the Connecticut Valley.

Hitchcock compared the foot of *Dinornis* with the fossil footprints he collected in the Connecticut Valley. The obvious similarities led him to conclude that birds like *Dinornis* had once existed in the valley in great numbers and made many of the footprints. It was only at the end of Hitchcock's life and after his death that the footprints were recognized as dinosaurian. Owen's description of *Archaeopteryx* in 1863, along with Cope's 1869 restudy of *Anchisaurus* bones that Hitchcock had collected in Springfield, Massachusetts, in 1855, showed the tracks were the marks of early dinosaurs similar to *Podokesaurus* and *Anchisaurus*.

Hitchcock made many great contributions to geology and paleontology in the Connecticut Valley, but still suffers the ignominy of being

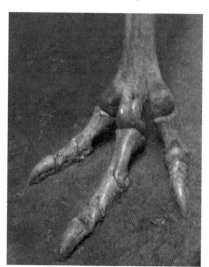

The foot of Dinornis
Courtesy of the Peabody Museum of Natural History, Yale University, New Haven, CT

remembered for having mistakenly identified local fossil footprints as those of large flightless birds. Although Hitchcock was among the first in a long line of paleontologists to encounter similarities between reptiles and birds, he is better known for having flubbed the call on local dinosaurs.

All it takes is a quick look at the skeleton of the large flightless bird Owen identified as *Dinornis* to see why Hitchcock reached the conclusion that he did. Rather than having blundered, it shows he may instead have been way ahead of his time. Take a good look at the feet of *Dinornis* and then walk all the way back, past *Apatosaurus*, to the dinosaur footprints arranged on the floor just before it. This exhibit is made of at least 16 different slabs designed to give visitors an idea of the various tracks found in the Connecticut Valley. Among them are the distinctive, three-toed, Connecticut Valley theropod footprints known as *Grallator* and *Eubrontes*. See how the *Eubrontes* track is a near perfect fit for the foot of *Dinornis*.

They may appear to be a very close match, close enough certainly to see why Hitchcock thought that the "true thunder" beast of the Connecticut Valley was a giant bird. "Birds inherited their foot structure directly from theropod dinosaurs," says paleontologist Paul Olsen. "Modern birds have modified [the design] a fair amount, but the earliest forms of birds, such as *Archaeopteryx*, have a foot indistinguishable from that of many contemporary dinosaurs.

"The basic three-toed foot structure," Paul emphasizes, "which looks so different from a mammal's, is literally a mark of dinosaurs. It's bipedal and has three forward-pointing toes. That says dinosaur. Nothing else has developed that formula."

Early ornithischians & later models

Make your way back past *Dinornis* to where the skeletons of several ornithischian dinosaurs are displayed. At the end of the Great Hall are the ceratopsians, including *Triceratops*. On the wall behind them is *Edmontosaurus*, one of the so-called duck-billed dinosaurs. Across the aisle, at the end of the center island, is the popular favorite, *Stegosaurus*. The mount is a composite of at least five individual dinosaurs and is now known to have too many pairs of spikes on its tail. Paleontologist Jim Farlow says Marsh "opened our eyes to the range of body form and the sheer exuberance of species of dinosaurs." The ornithischian dinosaurs illustrate his point best of all.

The ornithischians grew to include many fantastic forms of dinosaurs that thrived in Late Jurassic and Cretaceous times for well over a hundred million years and were the more numerous of the two orders of dinosaurs. The footprints Edward Hitchcock named *Anomoepus* are evidence that small primitive ornithischian dinosaurs lived in the Connecticut Valley long before, in Early Jurassic time. They were then only turkey sized and probably lacked the plates and spikes, armor and horns that adorned later ornithischians.

The differences between this small animal and the much larger and more exotic forms that field crews collected for Marsh from the American West offer another example of how dinosaurs changed and evolved from early forms similar to Connecticut Valley dinosaurs to the giants that appeared later.

New ideas: The legacy of curator John Ostrom

Jim Farlow remembers lying in bed one morning while a graduate student at Yale when an idea struck him. "Basically, I was not wanting to go to the lab and trying to convince myself I was sick and an idea just popped into my head: *Stegosaur's* plates were for temperature regulation!" Jim recalls.

It wasn't that he had a fever or needed to regulate his own body temperature; the thought just popped into his head. "I was so excited I immediately went into the Peabody collection and pulled out a *Stegosaurus* plate and saw that it was grooved for blood vessels, which it had to be for my idea to be plausible. So, I took it up and showed it to John Ostrom and told him my idea." Ostrom was then curator of the Peabody and an important leader in dinosaur science. Jim asked Ostrom if he could saw open a plate to see if the internal structure conformed to his expectation. "He said, 'Fine. Let's go for it,'" Jim recalls. It did and the rest is paleontological history. "John created an environment where it was just so exciting to be working on dinosaurs."

During the 1960s and 1970s, Ostrom brought new energy to dinosaur science, fueled in part by his own discovery of the small theropod dinosaur he named *Deinonychus*. This skeleton can be seen in an agile, aggressive, leaping position across the aisle from the skeleton of *Stegosaurus* in the Great Hall.

Deinonychus and the dinosaur-bird link

Ostrom imagined dinosaurs in new ways, and you can see it in his mount of *Deinonychus*. This small meat-eating, theropod dinosaur is posed like a living, breathing, active animal compared with older, less realistic style mounts such as the one Lull supervised of *Apatosaurus*.

Expeditions Ostrom led to the Cloverly Formation of Montana uncovered a collection of at least four *Deinonychus* skeletons in the mid-1960s. Judging from the way they lay in association with fragments of a large plant-eater, *Tenontosaurus*, Ostrom came to see these small theropods as lethal predators. Their anatomy suggested they were capable of leaping at their prey, seizing them in their long forearms and then finishing them off by slashing with the large and "terrible claws" of their feet.

The discovery of *Deinonychus* led Ostrom to view some dinosaurs as smarter and more agile than had been thought. He wondered if these theropods might have been warm-blooded and might have hunted in packs like modern-day wolves; in so doing, Ostrom changed the way many scientists and people thought about dinosaurs.

A few years later, Ostrom came across another fossil that struck him as remarkably similar to *Deinonychus*. Visiting a small museum in the Netherlands, he noticed a specimen that was identified as a flying reptile, that looked more like a small version of *Deinonychus* than a pterosaur. It was soon clear the fossil was actually the fourth then known specimen of *Archaeopteryx*, the earliest recognized bird.

Cast of Archaeopteryx
Courtesy of the Peabody Museum of Natural History, Yale University, New Haven, CT

Its similarity to *Deinonychus* led Ostrom to resurrect an earlier hypothesis of a possible link between dinosaurs and birds. The report he later published, *Archaeopteryx and the Origin of Birds*, was the most convincing case yet made for the theory that birds were descendants of theropods like *Deinonychus*.

Deinonychus
Copyright©2004,
Peabody Museum of Natural History,
Yale University, New Haven, CT

Ostrom's successor as curator at the Peabody, Jacques Gauthier, using a different approach to classification, has since provided evidence to argue that birds are more than descendants. They are actually surviving theropod dinosaurs. He and others suspect that the way theropods like *Deinonychus* used their arms to seize prey in a swooping motion may have been similar to the way early birds first began to flap their wings.

Yesterday & today at the Peabody

The Peabody has ranked as one of the most important natural history museums in the world since the day philanthropist George Peabody donated funds for its construction in 1866. The first building opened a decade later near the center of the Yale campus. The present museum first opened its doors in 1925. An excellent display of the museum's history and contributions to dinosaur science can be seen on the first landing of the stair to the upper floors. Here materials about the contributions of Peabody, Marsh, and collectors who worked for Marsh are on display.

Hanging above the second landing in the stairwell is a portrait of philanthropist George Peabody, Marsh's generous uncle. Look closely at the painting and a small portrait of Queen Victoria can be seen on the table next to Peabody. This small painting was a gift to Peabody from the queen in appreciation for his charitable work in England.

The museum continues to be an invaluable resource for paleontology. It hosts a constant stream of paleontologists from around the world who come to New Haven to examine the tens of thousands of fossils in its collections. The museum is staffed by specialists who are not only trained in paleontology, but skilled at everything from collecting fossils, to preparing fossils, to managing the collections.

Paleontologist Dan Brinkman has the job everyone who loves dinosaurs dreams of having. He is Assistant Collection Manager in Vertebrate Paleontology at the Peabody. Dan's office is routinely filled with rare dinosaur fossils and important old documents. When it comes to the Peabody, you might say he knows where all the bones are buried. Dan's job is to help collect and maintain not only specimens, but their records as well. Specimens that lack proper documentation lose much of their scientific value.

This book would not have been possible without Dan's many contributions. He shared his knowledge of the history of dinosaur science in the Connecticut Valley and the world. Dan painstakingly researched, edited and checked tremendous amounts of information for the book—while continuing to perform his usual duties, such as assisting visiting paleontologists with the museum's collection.

Marilyn Fox uncovers the secrets of fossils buried in stone. She is Chief Fossil Preparator at the Peabody and an expert at getting fossils ready for examination or display. It was Marilyn who took the call from Paul Olsen in 1996 when he needed help preparing the bones of *Erpetosuchus* that he discovered in Cheshire, Connecticut. She carefully cleared away millions of years worth of sandstone that surrounded his find. It is Marilyn's dream to see the dinosaurs of the Connecticut Valley get their own, special display in the museum.

In addition to the contributions Dan and Marilyn make to dinosaur science each day, they made invaluable contributions to this book—largely because of the passion they bring to the study of Connecticut dinosaurs.

Portland & Middletown, CT 11

Otozoum footprints installed in a wall at the Portland Library

Many of the earliest discoveries of dinosaur footprints were likely made in Connecticut Valley brownstone quarries. The history of stone quarrying and of fossil discoveries made in local quarries can still be explored around Portland and Middletown, Connecticut. Located on either side of the Connecticut River, multiple sites are easily visited in a few hours, including stops at the Portland brownstone quarries, the Portland Public Library in Portland, and Wesleyan University and the Indian Hill Cemetery in Middletown.

How to get there: The Portland brownstone quarries are located in Portland, Connecticut, west of Main Street and south of Middlesex Avenue (north of the bridge, and east of Brownstone Avenue). The north and south quarries are on either side of Silver Street. Follow Main Street and turn onto Silver Street. At the bottom of the hill, turn right onto Brownstone Avenue. Park along the retaining wall next to the larger, north quarry. Walking trails, including some with river views, can be reached by continuing on to the end of Brownstone Avenue.

The site

The Portland quarries were abandoned after the hurricane of 1938, and are now owned by the City of Portland. They have been preserved as historic sites. Brownstone has been quarried at Portland since early colonists settled along the river here in the mid-1600s. Known to geologists as arkose, and commonly seen in red sandstone layers throughout the valley, brownstone's rust red color comes from the iron oxides cemented within.

Geologist Greg McHone says that before quarry operations began there was a hill of brownstone behind the quarry that reached high overhead and to the river. Colonists made use of it at first by simply hauling off chunks scattered around on the ground. The stone was plentiful, easy to quarry and transport.

As demand increased, quarrying operations grew. Greg explains quarrying was done by first splitting the stone into thick slabs along bedding planes. These were the layers in which the sediments were originally deposited as gravel on river bottoms during Jurassic time. The slabs were then cut into blocks with huge saws.

The brownstone beds of the Portland quarries had the advantage of being nearly horizontal, unlike other sediment layers in the valley. Here they were folded and flattened. Sediments elsewhere are tilted ten or 15 degrees toward the eastern border fault. The Portland quarries, Greg says, must be part of a large block of the earth's upper crust that separated from tilted blocks by faults.

Sediments & natural resources

Besides abundance and ease of transport, brownstone also has the unique quality of being relatively soft when freshly cut. It is easy to carve at first and then later dries or cures to a harder, more brittle stone. This quality made brownstone highly desirable as a building material. The large hill of brownstone that once existed at the Portland Quarry was used to construct buildings, monuments, and bridges in the northeastern states and in New York City, where rows of the famous brownstone houses were built in the late nineteenth century. Many survive today as landmarks.

The quarries were abandoned after the hurricane of 1938 filled them with floodwaters. Demand for brownstone had by then declined and the storm was just the last straw. The water level in the quarries is now close to that of the river.

At least one section of quarry has since reopened in response to renewed demand for stone to repair and renovate aging structures, as well as for new construction. Brownstone is again being cut in an area behind the trees to the north of the old quarry.

Many different kinds of fossils have been found in similar brownstone quarries once common in the valley. Dinosaur footprints and natural casts of bones and plants were once so common in Portland brownstone that quarrymen came to regard them as flaws. Many were ignored and destroyed. Some were saved in museums and private collections.

"A remarkable 60-foot-long *Otozoum* trackway was found in the Portland Quarry in 1874," Rich Krueger reports. "It was the subject of a field trip of an American Association for the Advancement of Science meeting. A section was removed and displayed at a stonecutter's shop in Hartford and was later purchased for the Hartford Public High School where it is now

Anchisauripus footprints installed in a wall at the Portland Library

on display. Another section went to Wesleyan University and they donated it to Dinosaur State Park [where that section is now displayed]. The park's specimen is fabulous; you can clearly see skin impressions of the skin on the underside of the dinosaur's foot in the footprints."

The Portland Library

There are still footprints to be found in Portland, including a few installed at the Portland Library. The library is located just up the hill from the quarries, off Freestone Avenue and behind the police station. Inside the library there are two brownstone slabs. One contains several good quality, medium-size theropod footprints labeled as *Anchisauripus*. The other contains two remarkable specimens of *Otozoum*. Look closely and impressions of the skin of the underside of the trackmakers' foot can be clearly seen.

The Exley Science Center at Wesleyan University

More Portland Quarry footprints can be seen just across the river in Middletown, in the lobby of the science library at Wesleyan University. To reach Wesleyan, travel west across the bridge and the river, following Route 66. In Middletown, turn left on High Street and right on Church. The Exley Science Center is on the corner of Church and Pine.

Many footprints from the quarry are mounted on the walls

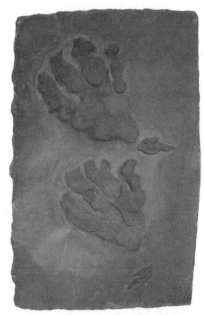

Otozoum & Grallator tracks at Wesleyan's Exley Center

of the science center's south lobby. There are several specimens of *Otozoum*, *Eubrontes* and *Grallator*. Other specimens found at local quarries can be seen at the Hartford Public High School in Hartford.

Also at the Exley Science Center is the Joe Webb Peoples Museum. Located on the fourth floor, it exhibits collections of fossils from around the world and Connecticut. The museum also displays many local minerals. Joe Webb Peoples was a central figure in Connecticut earth science for decades. As Director of the Connecticut State Geological and Natural History Survey, he contributed much to the knowledge about the state and was one of a small group of local scientists, elected officials and citizens who worked to protect the fossils at Dinosaur State Park after their discovery in 1966. Peoples was a founder of The Friends of Dinosaur Park & Arboretum, with Josephine Newton of Manchester, Connecticut. This group carries on the important work of protecting and preserving the park today.

The grave marker of Dr. Joseph Barrett

The Indian Hill Cemetery is located just west of Wesleyan, at the corner of Vine Street and Route 66 in Middletown. The unique gravestone of Dr. Joseph Barrett, one of Connecticut's most accomplished amateur fossil hunters, is toward the west of the cemetery hilltop.

There has always been room for amateurs in the Connecticut Valley's tradition of dinosaur science. The truth is that ordinary folk have made many of the most significant discoveries in the valley in the past two hundred years, from the time Pliny Moody dug up the footprints of *Noah's Raven* with horse and plow to the day Edward McCarthy jumped down off his bulldozer to inspect the tracks he uncovered at Dinosaur State Park.

Barrett was a medical doctor known for his great love of science, especially geology and botany. Living in Middletown, he was well acquainted with local brownstone quarries, including the

217

quarries that were recently designated as historic sites just across the river in Portland, and the fossils found there.

The earliest discoveries?

Among Barrett's most impressive discoveries was a piece of paving stone recovered from the streets of Middletown and later sold to Edward Hitchcock. While Hitchcock generally attributed the earliest discovery of fossil footprints in the Connecticut Valley to Pliny Moody, the stone Barrett collected is likely evidence that local quarrymen were finding footprints decades earlier.

Middletown residents trod on the stone, Barrett estimated, for more than half a century. When it finally was replaced, after many years of service, he made a dramatic discovery. Its underside was covered by dozens of very high-quality fossil footprints.

Even more remarkable was that the stone was likely quarried long before the tracks of *Noah's Raven* were uncovered in 1802. By Barrett's estimate, the stone was cut years earlier, during the American Revolution—perhaps a quarter century before Pliny Moody made his discovery.

"This slab, of slightly reddish micaceous sandstone, has been used as a flagging stone in the streets of Middletown for sixty years," Hitchcock wrote in 1858. "Fifteen or twenty years ago it was taken up, when the tracks were discovered on the other side, and it was secured by Dr. Joseph Barrett, who thus early had become much interested in footmarks, and from him I purchased it for the Ichnological Cabinet. It was dug from the quarry about two miles west of the city, as Dr. Barrett supposes, nearly eighty years ago; but at present that quarry exhibits no sign of any such tracks, and scarcely of any other."

Steve Sauter says Hitchcock considered the stone the "gem" of his collection. Its discovery was just one of many contributions Barrett made to Hitchcock's work and to the science of ichnology.

The gravestones of Dr. Joseph Barrett

Curious about curiosities

Barrett was in many ways ahead of his time in searching local brownstone quarries for fossils and in seeking to understand their meaning. He collected many rocks and fossils throughout the valley and had a great ability to imagine how they came to be preserved. Some of his ideas were fanciful, others shrewdly insightful. It was because of his insights that he remains a figure of note.

Barrett began picking over local fossils when most were still unknown. He wrote to Benjamin Silliman about several he found at the Portland quarries in 1836, roughly the same time Edward Hitchcock made his first report of fossil tracks from the north valley. Through their common interests, Barrett and Hitchcock began a correspondence. Hitchcock referred to Barrett frequently and later named footprints for him, but sometimes misspelled his friend's name, as he was wont to do.

Barrett came to develop an intuitive sense for local fossils and the ways in which they were preserved. In some cases, they led him to significant conclusions. He recognized how animals and even plants could be fossilized by dissolution and replacement, for example, before the process was well known: "Dr. Barrett has made a suggestion in conversation, in regard to the fossilization of the bones of these ancient animals, which seems deserving consideration," Hitchcock wrote. "He supposes that he has found numerous specimens of the petrified bones of huge animals in the quarries around Middletown. But there is no bony matter, or none of consequence, remaining. There seems to have been an entire substitution of sandstone for organic matter. It is obvious that where the mere form is all we have to judge from, there is large room for the play of imagination.

"Yet I confess," Hitchcock continued, "that one or two specimens, pointed out to me by Dr. Barrett, seemed so closely to imitate a group of large vertebrae, as to deserve attention. For it is a fact, that nearly all of the vegetable organic remains in the Connecticut River sandstone, do not retain any of the original vegetable matter, but seem to be mere casts, formed by filling up the moulds once occupied by the plant, with sand and such, sometimes coarser than the surrounding rock.

"Witness, for instance, the huge trunks of trees from the Portland quarries in the Geological Cabinet of Amherst College, and the smaller ones from Newark, New Jersey," Hitchcock went on to observe. "Why may not a like mode of fossilization have taken place with bones? At Springfield, (Mass.) they are, indeed, entirely changed into carbonate of lime; and at Ketch's Mills ['the Bones from the Well'], they are preserved, having lost only their animal matter.

"If these suggestions should prove true, they may explain the reason why we find so few of the bones of these ancient animals," Hitchcock concluded. "For in the first place, if such is the nature of this sandstone, or such were the circumstances attending its consolidation, that even bones would often entirely disappear and leave only a mould, how seldom would the mould have been so filled that the cast should be recognized as that of a bone; and secondly, since we have not sought for such a kind of petrification of bones, perhaps by looking for them at the quarries, they may not unfrequently be found, as Dr. Barrett supposes he has done."

In other cases, Barrett's intuitions proved less reliable. "I am aware that Dr. Joseph Barrett. . . who has paid great attention to this subject for more than twenty years, maintains that he has discovered frost marks in the sandstone," Hitchcock noted about one of Barrett's theories he found unlikely. From what Hitchcock had learned of red sandstone, it was an indication of a hot, tropical world, not the sort of climate that got cold enough for a freeze. Hitchcock offered an alternate explanation. "[Dr. Barrett] has kindly shown me his specimens, which may, indeed, have had such an origin. But they do not seem to me to require any other agency than water, and perhaps Annelids [worms], for their production."

Barrett's memorial

Following Barrett's death in 1882, friends erected a truly unique headstone in his honor. On its face the stone reads, "JOSEPH BARRETT, M. D. BOTANIST, GEOLOGIST." Numerous theropod dinosaur footprints can be seen on the back of stone, along with sandstone casts of the trunks of several Jurassic trees, inscribed, "THE TESTIMONY OF THE ROCKS."

The Hitchcock Collection 12

Moody's Trackway
Pratt Museum of Natural History at Amherst College

The Hitchcock Ichnological Collection is one of the most important collections of dinosaur footprints that exists in the world today. It was assembled between 1835 and 1864 by one of the greatest paleontologists ever to work in the Connecticut Valley, Edward Hitchcock. His collection contains as many as 20,000 specimens of trace fossils, mostly dinosaur footprints. It frames a unique chapter in the history of the study of the ancient world.

How to arrange a visit to the collection: An appointment is required to see the collection. The Pratt Museum of Natural History Museum at Amherst College has closed while plans for a new museum are being made, but small groups may still schedule appointments to tour the Hitchcock Collection. For information about how to schedule an appointment, visit the Amherst College web site for the Pratt Museum.

How to get there: The Hitchcock Collection is located on the Amherst College campus in Amherst, Massachusetts. From I-91, take the exit for Route 9/Amherst. Follow Route 9 east into Amherst. Metered parking is available downtown along the Common, just past the intersection with Route 116. The collection is located just a short walk across the street from the Common, at the southeast corner of the Amherst College Quadrangle, in the basement of the former Pratt Museum. Tours of the Hitchcock Collection are by appointment only.

Introduction

Long before there were dinosaur museums, Edward Hitchcock began one of the most unique collections of dinosaur fossils in the world today. During his tenure as professor of natural history, and later as president of Amherst College, Hitchcock was able to use the fossils to piece together an astonishing picture of the valley as it was some 200 million years ago. The collection is significant not only for what it reveals of life early in the age of dinosaurs, but also for the role it played in the development of scientific inquiry in the young American republic.

The legacy of Edward Hitchcock

"Yet, I hope it will not be forgotten," Hitchcock wrote, "that on this subject [of fossil footprints] I have had to find out my way alone, almost unaided by previous researches. This fact, ought, I think, to secure me some indulgence of criticism, especially when the peculiar difficulties of the subject are taken into account."

Peculiar difficulties abounded. At the time Hitchcock began his work in 1836, dinosaurs were essentially unknown to science. It was not until 1842 that the English anatomist Richard Owen first described three, extinct reptiles as dinosaurs. Strange fossil footprints, however, were known from the Connecticut Valley at least forty years earlier, and likely well before. No one had any idea what a dinosaur was or knew much at all about the world in the ancient past.

Hitchcock was indeed alone when he began his explorations of the footprints and traces of the Connecticut Valley. There was little or no previous experience to draw upon with regard to fossil traces of animals such as footprints. Most geologists of the time dismissed footprints as indistinct, geological oddities without scientific value.

Leptodactylous footprint
Pratt Museum of Natural History
at Amherst College

What was known of prehistoric animals was being learned primarily from fossil bones being studied by scientists like Owen across the Atlantic in England. The United States was then comparatively isolated. Memories of the Revolutionary War were still fresh in the minds of many. In Hitchcock's family, both his father and grandfather had soldiered against the British, and his grandfather had perished in the squalor of the winter camps.

Hitchcock himself suffered from chronic illnesses most of his life. It was a struggle for him to read or work. Yet, he prevailed to single-handedly invent the field of ichnology (the study of fossil footprints). He established standards for inquiry and identified hundreds of species of footprints. His work has stood as an essential resource for the field ever since.

The early museum & the Appleton Cabinet

The first natural history museum at Amherst was built in 1848 and came to be known as the Octagon. Hitchcock worked to add to the college's collection with donations of minerals and fossils from alumni, many of whom were active in related fields. The specimens were used as teaching aids in the college's science classes.

A group of local supporters, including notables Samuel Appleton, Edward and William Dickinson, Jonathon Phillips and

Interior of the Appleton Cabinet
Courtesy, Steve Sauter

Samuel Williston, donated time, money and specimens to construct a building designed for housing and exhibiting the Hitchcock Collection in 1855. Hitchcock also listed Plinius and Pliny Moody as donors in recognition of discoveries made at their farm, including the footprints of *Noah's Raven* found fifty years earlier.

Named for Appleton, who donated the sum of $10,000 for its construction, the building was sited on the southwest corner of the College Quadrangle. (The building has since had a third floor added and been converted into a dormitory.) The location allowed sunlight to pour through the building's tall windows much of the day. Its exposure also had the advantage of providing angular light of the sort that was invaluable in examining fossil footprints.

Noah's Raven
Amherst College catalog number AC 16/2

The earliest recorded discovery of a dinosaur fossil in North America was that of a slab of sandstone said to contain the tracks of *Noah's Raven,* in about 1802 (photo on page 21). "So strikingly did these tracks resemble those of birds," Hitchcock wrote, "that they were familiarly spoken of as the tracks of 'poultry' or of 'Noah's Raven.'"

As the story goes, Pliny Moody plowed up the stone while working the fields at the Moody family farm in South Hadley, Massachusetts, just down the road from Amherst College. The stone itself isn't big, nor are the tracks raised in relief on its surface. They are recognized today as the footprint *Anomoepus*, probably the tracks of a small plant-eating, ornithischian dinosaur.

Moody's trackway
Amherst College catalog number AC 3/1

This colossal trackway was removed in pieces from the Moody farm and put back together as a composite (photo page 223). It is shown in a lithograph that Hitchcock published in his 1858 report on the geology and ichnology of the Connecticut Valley. The trackway contains many remarkable specimens of the footprint *Otozoum moodii,* which Hitchcock named for Pliny Moody, along with several smaller footprints of the type known as *Grallator.*

Otozoum footprints were probably made by an early form of medium-sized, plant-eating, prosauropod dinosaur. It walked on two feet leaving impressions of four large toes. It would also sometimes rest with its forefeet on the ground. Impressions of its hands are rare, but some have been preserved.

"*Otozoum* tracks look bigger than they really are," says Paul Olsen. "The foot implants not just the toes, but all the way up to the ankle. The footprint is as big as *Eubrontes*, but if you scaled it to the same part of the foot it wouldn't be as big, so the animal wasn't very big."

The stone book

Hitchcock paid attention to the details of footprints and the way they were displayed in his cabinet. He sought the help of local blacksmiths to fashion display tables and his "stone book."

The stone book was made to show how a footprint may be impressed on or through several layers of mud and how the appearance of a single footprint changes from one layer to another. It clearly shows the difference between true tracks, over tracks and under tracks. In muddy conditions, a dinosaur could leave several impressions while making just a single step. The "true track" was the more accurate mold of the animal's foot compared with distorted impressions left above (the "over track") or below (the "under track").

Hitchcock's stone book contains two examples of a footprint he named *Platyperna*, and attributed to "thin-toed" birds. Hitchcock described many examples of strangely shaped, thin-toed footprints and classified them as *Leptodactylous* footprints. Most were thought for years to be poorly preserved impressions or under tracks. "The idea was that the dinosaur would walk along and he would step on one layer, or she would step on one layer, and that track would be impressed on the layer underneath in a more vague sense," says Paul Olsen. Steve Sauter has his tour groups imagine stepping on a pile of blankets as an example.

The stone book
Pratt Museum of Natural History
at Amherst College

Recently, Hitchcock's stone book and his *Leptodactylous* tracks have taken on greater meaning. Studies of theropod dinosaur footprints discovered in Greenland by biologist Stephen Gatesy have expanded previous concepts of under tracks.

Steve has shown how footprints made in deep mud may be more than just vague impressions of the undersides of dinosaur feet. In some cases, tracks Hitchcock identified as *Leptodactylous* may actually be a different sort of fossil record altogether.

Steve's computer animations show how the shapes of deep footprints are consistent with his theory of how theropod dinosaurs walked. Deep impressions can preserve a three-dimensional record of the motion of a dinosaur's foot during the time (the fourth dimension) it took for the animal to walk through the mud.

The *Eubrontes* type specimen
Amherst College catalog number AC 15/3

This footprint was the first one Edward Hitchcock identified as *Eubrontes* and is known as the "type specimen." It is an extraordinary fossil in a collection full of extraordinary fossils.

Eubrontes is a favorite of ichnologists, including Paul Olsen. Rich Krueger calls it "the coolest footprint in the valley."

The four-quart *Eubrontes* footprint
Amherst college catalog nos. 15/1, 45/1 & others

"How amazed should we be to meet flocks of such birds now?" Hitchcock once asked of the large, flightless birds he believed were the makers of the large footprints he named *Eubrontes*. He imagined them to have had certain nobility as they raced through the valley like a herd of spirited war horses, relentlessly in motion.

Eubrontes type specimen
Courtesy, Paul E. Olsen

229

Hitchcock found the size of their footprints astounding, often measuring the impressions by filling them with water. "One from Northampton, No. 15/1, will hold four quarts of water," he noted. The specimen is just as impressive today.

The *Eubrontes* footprint is recognized today as unmistakably the mark of a large, meat-eating, theropod dinosaur. Paul Olsen believes they appeared suddenly following a mass extinction at the end of Triassic time, to put new bite in the definition of large, predatory dinosaurs. They were not as large as *Tyrannosaurus rex*, but twice as large as any of the small theropods that lived in the Triassic or that were known from the valley, including the skeleton of *Podokesaurus* found nearby, in Holyoke, Massachusetts.

Even more frightening is the fact that their footprints are among the most common in the valley. There weren't just a few that stayed to the fringes of large herds of plant-eaters, like a pride of lions. These beasts existed in large numbers—and likely snapped at anything that moved. They could run perhaps ten miles an hour and cover four or five feet with one stride.

Steve Sauter tells the story of one visitor who seemed particularly startled by seeing these footprints. "Is something wrong?" Steve was moved to inquire. "No," the woman told him, "it's just that we have those on our farm—and I never knew what they were before!" Her realization that meat-eating dinosaurs of such proportions once prowled the north valley—and her fields—was overwhelming.

The four-quart footprint
Pratt Museum of Natural History
at Amherst College

Pads, feet and bones
Amherst College catalog number 49/1

Two people who have spent as much time as anyone studying

the collection in recent years are Paul Olsen and Emma Rainforth. Carrying on the work begun by Hitchcock is an enormous undertaking, but those who devote their time to it are still rewarded with exciting results.

For starters, there are a great many species and names of tracks that must be sorted through, more than there ought to be, given what has been learned about dinosaurs in recent years. Straightening things out requires both knowledge of the rules Hitchcock used to classify footprints, and of new approaches that have been developed since. And it requires patience. It takes time to measure footprints, especially those that are poorly preserved, making it hard to be sure exactly where a footprint begins or ends.

The most useful footprints are those that preserve impressions of the pads of the feet. The round bulges or pads on the underside of the foot generally correspond to joints between toe bones. If impressions of toes and pads are well enough preserved, they may allow an approximation of the trackmaker's foot to be drawn. This can then be compared with actual dinosaur feet known from fossil bones. It may not be precise enough to positively identify the trackmaker, but can help to eliminate dinosaurs that don't make a good fit.

Some footprints in the collection still show the white paint Paul used to delineate the shapes of footprints, including the toes and pads. One slab, the specimen marked AC 49/1 for example, is impressed with tracks of *Grallator* footprints. It includes the shapes of toes and pads.

Grallator footprints
Pratt Museum of Natural History
at Amherst College

Dr. Barrett's Middletown paving stone
Amherst College catalog number 19/4

Steve Sauter says that Hitchcock called the paving stone Dr. Joseph Barrett gave him "the gem" of the collection. It's easy to see why. Framed in wood and stood on end behind a beautiful, white marble bust of Hitchcock, the underside of the stone is covered with extraordinarily high-quality footprints (photo on page 19).

Besides the stone's remarkable state of preservation—given the fact it was laid impression side down and used as a paving stone in Middletown, Connecticut for many years—the stone may be significant for another reason. Barrett estimated the stone was quarried at Middletown many years before it was laid as a paving stone, perhaps as early as 1780. If so, the stone is decades older than *Noah's Raven*, and would be one of the earliest verifiable discoveries of a dinosaur fossil in the world.

The mysteries of *Anomoepus*
Amherst College catalog number AC 48/1 & others

Paul and Emma have also made extensive studies of the *Anomoepus* footprints in the collection. Through their efforts, these footprints have been shown to occur widely throughout the world in the Early Jurassic and have come to serve as an international standard for identifying similar footprints found in the American West, Europe and Africa.

Anomoepus is known not just by the impressions of feet, but also for the impressions of forelimbs or hands. Hitchcock gave this species of tracks the name "unlike foot," because of the puzzle the impressions presented. It includes three-toed impressions of the rear feet, like a turkey's, often accompanied by smaller, five-toed impressions of forefeet. The puzzle was, if these were the marks of birds, what sort of bird might have had hands?

Paul says the handprints are a sign that *Anomoepus* was made by a primitive form of ornithischian dinosaur. It was a turkey-sized plant-eater, with a small head, long tail and relatively long limbs.

Anomoepus
Pratt Museum of Natural History at Amherst College

another footprint.

Anomoepus footprints also suggest the trackmaker was gregarious, as later ornithischian dinosaurs are sometimes known to have been. Footprints of several individuals of different sizes are not unusual. There are stones that include footprints of such different sizes that Paul thinks they show the presence of families of dinosaurs, indicating that the trackmakers of *Anomoepus* cared for their young.

Raindrops & tadpoles

Also in the collection are many remarkable trace fossils. Two of Steve Sauter's favorites are stones marked as numbers 28/6 and 38/19. Number 28/6 preserves 200 million-year-old raindrops that look like they're still fresh, while number 38/19 shows what Hitchcock described as traces of tadpoles left in the banks of the Connecticut River.

"Such was the fauna of the Connecticut Valley. What a wonderful menagerie! Who would believe that such a register lay buried in the strata? To open the leaves, to unroll the papyrus, has been an intensely interesting though difficult work, having all the excitement and marvelous developments of romance. And yet the volume is only partly

read. Many a new page I fancy will yet be opened, and many a new key obtained to the hieroglyphic record. I am thankful that I have been allowed to see so much by prying between the folded leaves. At first men supposed that the strange and gigantic races which I had described, were mere creatures of imagination, like the Gorgons and Chimeras of the ancient poets. But now that hundreds of their footprints, as fresh and distinct as if yesterday impressed upon the mud, arrest the attention of the sceptic on the ample slabs of our cabinets, he might as reasonably doubt his own corporeal existence as that of these enormous and peculiar races."

—Edward Hitchcock

Mount Tom Footprints 13

One of the oldest known footprint sites that remains easily accessible is the Dinosaur Footprints Reservation, located near the foot of Mount Tom in Holyoke, Massachusetts. It has been studied by paleontologists for centuries, since Edward Hitchcock first came to study tracks at this site. One of the footprints Hitchcock described from this site was the first to be named *Eubrontes*.

How to get there: Approximately one mile north of Holyoke, Massachusetts, and one-half mile east of the Mount Tom Recreation Area on Route 5. Going north on Route I-91, take Exit 17A (Route 141 East) towards Holyoke. Turn left onto Route 5 North and follow for 2.2 miles. There is a parking area on the right. Going south on Route I-91, take Exit 18 and follow Route 5 south toward Holyoke for 5.2 miles. The parking area is on the left. Open April 1 to November 30, sunrise to sunset.

The site

The Dinosaur Footprints Reservation is an area of tilted sandstone outcrops along the banks of the Connecticut River. These track-bearing sediments formed along the shoreline of an Early Jurassic lakefront. They record the movements of a large number of theropod dinosaurs and have fascinated paleontologists for over a century.

To reach the trackway, follow the walkway from the parking area as it parallels the roadway above. Continue through a short wooded section of the trail and the main trackway is visible straight ahead.

Were some dinosaurs gregarious?

One of the things Edward Hitchcock and others realized about fossil hunting in the Connecticut Valley—and for that matter most places in the world—is that it's best to look in places where nature and time have already done most of the digging for you.

Many of the fossil footprints Hitchcock collected were found along the banks and in the coves of the Connecticut River. Periodic floods made the river quite effective at exposing fossil-bearing sandstones and mudstones in its flood plain. Fewer of these types of places remain today since flood controls and dams have been constructed to control river levels.

The site is a must-visit for any number of reasons. It is one of the best places in the valley to experience a dinosaur in the same way paleontologists like Edward Hitchcock and John Ostrom experienced it. Hitchcock looked at the tracks here, most of which lead in a similar, generally westerly direction, and wondered if the animals that made them might not have moved together in groups or exhibited other social behavior.

"This indeed is the most abundant locality," Hitchcock wrote. "Here are found several parallel and some intersecting rows of this [*Eubrontes*] species of track, which often run oblique to what must have been the direction of the shore where they were made. These facts make the gregarious character of the animals probable."

The Mount Tom site drew John Ostrom's attention more than a century after Hitchcock wrote about it. Since discovering the remains of another theropod dinosaur, *Deinonychus*, in Montana in 1964, Ostrom had been intrigued by dinosaur behavior.

The collection of bones he found in Montana included at least four of the theropods, presumably predators, and a single larger plant-eater, apparently their prey. The remains suggested that at least four and probably more *Deinonychus* had pursued the herbivore *Tenontosaurus* as a pack, like modern-day wolves, acting in some sort of coordinated, group effort to overwhelm their prey.

The famous Mount Tom trackway in Holyoke, Massachusetts

Two years later, in 1966, the tracks at Dinosaur State Park in Rocky Hill, Connecticut, were uncovered. They were also evidence of large numbers of theropod dinosaurs traversing a lakeshore, but the generally random direction of those tracks didn't offer evidence of the animals moving as a group.

Ostrom returned to Mount Tom in 1970 to follow up on a hunch he had from his first visit to this spot. "Several years ago, I visited a well-known dinosaur footprint locality at Holyoke, Massachusetts. The site, known for many years to local residents, had not generated any special interest among paleontologists… I was somewhat surprised to observe that nearly all of the conspicuous trackways preserved at this site led in very nearly the same direction. I concluded that the site should be mapped carefully and studied in detail… During the summer of 1970, I was finally able to return to Holyoke and mapped the Mt. Tom site with steel tape and Brunton compass."

Ostrom divided the trackway into a five-foot square grid, measured the sizes and positions of the tracks and recorded the information on graph paper. He recorded a total of 134 footprints, including 28 track paths he attributed to the Connecticut Valley ichnospecies, *Eubrontes*, *Grallator* and *Anchisauripus*. Twenty of the 28 tracks he identified led in westerly directions. All were most likely *Eubrontes* trackways. Seven tracks did not lead in a westerly direction, including four tracks of the smaller ichnospecies, *Grallator* and *Anchisauripus*.

Ostrom used what is known as a rose diagram to plot the compass bearings and directions of the tracks. The method made it possible to quickly see a pattern in the fossil evidence. The results seemed to show a group of twenty large theropods moving together in a group or herd.

"It thus appears that the primary factor[s] responsible for the preferred orientation at the Mt. Tom site was taxonomically controlled," Ostrom concluded. "A group of 19 animals of the

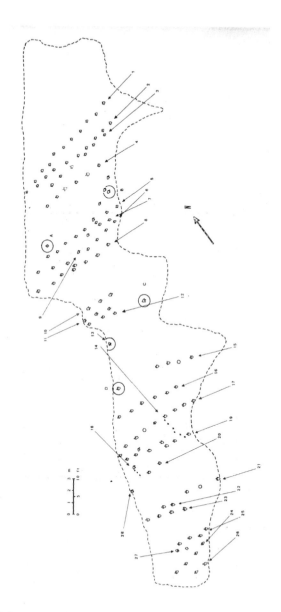

The map John Ostrom drew of the Mount Tom trackway

same kind, progressing together in the same direction, is best described as a herd. Other animal species in the area seem not to have been influenced by whatever caused the "*Eubrontes*" herd to migrate to the west...

"The only other possible explanation for non-random trackway patterns," Ostrom observed, "requires the presence of some sort of physical barrier at each site that created a natural corridor or otherwise funneled most of the traffic along a common path. The fact that divergent trackways do occur... weakens this explanation. The additional fact that these divergent tracks often are of a kind quite different from those in the preferred orientation, strongly suggests that the lineation resulted from taxonomic rather than external environmental influences."

The studies Ostrom made of this site, along with comparisons he made to others in Texas, Connecticut and England, marked an early effort to draw conclusions about dinosaur behavior from footprint evidence. He published his results in 1972 in a scientific paper entitled *Were Some Dinosaurs Gregarious?*

A current view

"I was very influenced by that paper," says Martin Lockley, "because Ostrom asked a very important question. Were the animals walking in a given direction because of what he called a physically controlled pathway? In other words, were they following along a corridor because of the landscape, like cattle being driven down a canyon or something? Or was this more of an inherent biological phenomenon of gregarious behavior, where these animals liked to congregate and travel together?

"It made me think about those two options," Martin continues. "It also led me to come up with a third. That is, it may not be a simple, either-or case. If you have animals that are gregarious they also are going to be likely to follow the natural routes of the landscape, and so it's very likely a combination of these factors.

One of the many Eubrontes footprints found at the Mount Tom site.

"I have been to the Mount Tom site and certainly the evidence is that these were carnivorous dinosaurs—theropod dinosaurs," Martin states. "I reviewed the evidence for dinosaur track sites that appeared to show gregarious behavior amongst theropods. They're still fairly rare. I think there are still only six or eight sites where we have clearly demarcated, parallel, theropod trackways, suggestive of gregarious behavior."

In his work out West, Martin has found a lot of footprint evidence to support the notion that some dinosaurs did indeed move in herds, but he isn't convinced theropod dinosaurs were among them. He's tempted to retrace Ostrom's steps and make a new study of the Mount Tom site himself one of these days. Regardless, he says the study Ostrom made here was among the first to show the utility of track evidence to answering questions of dinosaur behavior.

"One thing I believe we can say about theropods as opposed to all herbivorous dinosaurs was that their behavior was different in a qualitative way," Martin points out. "It is common to find evidence of ornithopods and sauropods that were gregarious and relatively rare amongst theropods.

"We have sites from the Late Jurassic and Cretaceous where not only do we have parallel trackways of ornithopods and sauropods, but there is an organic flow to them. These animals would all veer to the right and then they would all veer to the left and then they would all veer to the right again. These animals were moving like a single organism. I've never seen any hint of that in the theropods.

"I'm not passing judgment on theropods," he says, "but the behavior of these animals was more primitive and more inclined to be behavior patterns of individuals and less complex social

organization. There are certainly sites with multiple theropod trackways, but they seem to crisscross in random directions. They were probably coming to a watering hole or something from all directions, but there's no indication of ten or twenty of them going all in the same direction at one time."

Discovering footprints

The Mount Tom site is still a great place to experience dinosaur footprints directly. The sandstone has weathered, and some tracks are less distinct than others, but even an amateur can make out much of what Hitchcock and Ostrom observed.

Ostrom noticed that all of the footprints at the site were those of theropod dinosaurs. Distinguished generally in terms of their relative size, they are all what Paul Olsen and Emma Rainforth refer to as "Grallatorids." Grallatorids are all theropod footprints. Differences in size may be due to differences between individuals, whether trackmakers were males or females or juveniles or adults, rather than differences between families or types of theropods.

Ostrom identified the theropod footprints as belonging to three ichnogenera, *Eubrontes*, *Anchisauripus* and *Grallator*. It may be that the footprints are the marks of one of two kinds of Grallatorids, rather than three.

The greatest numbers of tracks leading in westerly directions (toward the retaining wall and the road) are *Eubrontes* footprints, made by the animal Hitchcock dubbed the "giant ruler of the valley." They are the largest footprints, measuring 11 to 14 inches from heel to toe and marking strides three to four feet long. The animals were moving at about five to 7-1/2 miles per hour.

A few of the tracks, notably those crossing in a generally southeasterly direction, are those of the smaller, *Grallator* type. This was the footprint Hitchcock called the "stilt walker." Their footprints measure 3-1/2 to five inches from heel to toe and they walked in strides of about one to two feet long.

Barton Cove 14

This beautiful cove along the Connecticut River is an excellent place to have a picnic and to experience the environment and physical conditions of sites that preserved fossil footprints. Paleontologists collected many trace fossils around Barton Cove in the past. Today, it is known more as a nesting site for the bald eagles that can be seen along the nearby river in late winter and early spring.

Few trace fossils remain and those that do may be difficult to distinguish, but the natural beauty of this place, its fun hiking trails and dramatic geology, make it a great place to explore a site that remains much as it was when Edward Hitchcock and others came here to look for footprints.

In many places, the cove still retains a prehistoric look and feel. There is no better way to experience what it was like to discover a fossil here than to walk along the water's edge or the trails.

How to get there: Going north on Route 1-91, take Exit 27 (Route 2 East). Follow Route 2 East for about three miles. Turn right into the driveway at the sign for the Barton Cove picnic and camping areas. Follow the driveway up to the main parking lot.

Barton Cove is affiliated with the Northfield Mountain Recreation and Environmental Center and is operated by Northeast Utilities. It is a day use area. Campground areas are open Memorial Day through Labor Day. Reservations are required.

Tilted layers of sandstone

Near the far end of the picnic area, and around the cove toward the camp areas, tilted outcrops of sandstone jut out into the water. Up the camp road and along the hiking trails, there are even bigger exposures of tilted layers of sandstone and brownstone— just the sorts of exposures early paleontologists looked for to find footprints.

These outcrops are often surrounded by tall coniferous trees and topped with wonderfully lush plant communities, including ferns, mosses and lichens, evocative of images of the ancient past. Along their faces, they reveal sections of the sediments of the northern Connecticut Valley in the familiar pattern of the thin-sliced layer cake. In places the layers are brittle and flaking apart as they weather and erode.

Look carefully at the outcrops along the water's edge. Partial footprints are still present and in some cases even retain partial impressions of the skin on the underside of the trackmaker's foot.

Tilted sandstone outcrops

Ripple marks

Look out over the water when there is a light breeze. Notice the rows of small waves that appear on the surface. The wind made the same pattern on the surface of lakes in Mesozoic time, some 200 million years ago. Examples of fossil ripple marks can still be found in some of the sandstone outcrops along the water's edge.

"Ripple marks are very frequently seen on the surface over which animals walked…" Edward Hitchcock wrote in his description. "From the ripple marks we learn the important fact, that the surface on which the animals trod, was a little time previously beneath the waters, and that the animals trod upon it

Large block of sandstone showing ripples and cracks

before it had been above the waters long enough to get hardened, or to have the ripple marks effaced.

"Yet, subsequently," Hitchcock continued, "and with no great interval of time, the spot must have again been beneath the water, in order to bring over it new layers of mud to be converted into rocks. That the interval was short appears from the perfection of the tracks, which, if long exposed to atmospheric influences, must have been wholly or partially erased."

Sun cracks and mud veins

Some ripple marks also show cracks in the sandstone casts that formed when the mud was later baked dry under the hot sun of a dry season. What seem like ordinary cracks have actually given paleontologists a better understanding of climate cycles in the Connecticut Valley during Mesozoic time.

"If a muddy and especially a clayey surface be long exposed without rain to a hot sun, it becomes filled with cracks, which generally run in such directions to form polygonal masses," Edward Hitchcock wrote. "The cracks are often quite deep, and if afterwards mud is brought over the spot by water, it falls into these fissures, so that when the whole is converted into rocks and split open, we shall have the surface covered with mud veins, which, though they meet and apparently intersect, never cut off one another, but coalesce at the crossings.

"These mud veins are very common in the shale of this valley," Hitchcock observed, "and to unpracticed eyes are quite perplexing. The most remarkable locality that I have ever seen is at the Portland quarries, where sometimes the surface looks like mosaic, or rather like a pavement of polygonal masses, with mortar between the pieces."

Environmental Responsibility 15

Watch people fishing these days and you will notice they do things differently than in the past. Many are taking a new approach to the sport they love, in part because it takes them outdoors and to beautiful locations. They practice *"catch and release"* fishing and do all they can to return fish to the water as quickly as possible, unharmed, immediately after reeling them in. Few take fish as trophies any more; they take photos instead.

Collect photos

It's a great idea and one amateur fossil hunters are coming to appreciate for its practicality as well. Photographs are simply the best way to keep a record of explorations or discoveries—especially since digital cameras have become easy to use, reliable and affordable.

Steve Sauter tells a story about going to the Natural History Museum in London with his family on vacation, where they found a fossil he had wanted for years to see. He and his son took digital pictures of it. On their way back to the hotel, they snapped some pictures of London. They weren't in their room long before Steve's son put several images together and emailed them to family and friends back home. He shared pictures of fossils Steve had waited years to see, with people across the world, in little more than the time it takes for a London cab to get from Kensington to Piccadilly.

Fossils discovered in the valley can be shared the same way. Taking photographs lets you take a souvenir of the experience home and leaves footprints or other relics of the ancient past as they were, unharmed and unchanged, for others to experience for generations to come. Start a collection of photographs and keep a record of where the photographs were taken, the time of day, the weather and the friends and family members who came along.

If you would like to photograph footprints at outdoor sites, get there when the sun is lower in the sky rather than high above. Plan a trip for the early morning or late afternoon, when the sun is long, and casts shadows across trackways. Footprints are not only more easily seen when there are shadows, they photograph better as well.

Never use chalk to outline or mark a footprint. Never make casts of any kind. Even experienced paleontologists are reluctant to do anything that may damage a footprint. Most techniques work only with certain prints or under special circumstances. They can ruin tracks and in the process destroy their scientific value forever. Never take a fossil from any location. It's illegal to take rocks, minerals or fossils from public land; on private lands it's theft.

Make casts at Dinosaur State Park, Connecticut

If you want a dinosaur footprint of your own, it's easy. Go to the casting area at Dinosaur State Park early on a weekday morning. You will have the place to yourself and can enjoy a picnic sitting in Rich Krueger's magnificent arboretum while you wait for the plaster to harden—no muss, no fuss. In less than an hour, you'll have a very high-quality, *Eubrontes* footprint of your own, one much better than can be made anywhere else in the entire valley.

Be a hero

If you do find something that looks significant—don't move it! Be a hero instead. The best thing to do is to call the Vertebrate Paleontology Department at the Peabody Museum, just as the Baron boys did after they found the chunk of brownstone containing fossils of *Hypsognathus*, and ask for help.

Remember, many of the most important discoveries ever made in the valley were made by amateurs like Pliny Moody and Edward McCarthy. McCarthy earned his place in history by shutting down his bulldozer and calling for help before he did anything that might damage what he'd uncovered—even before he knew what it was. As a result of his quick thinking, tens of thousands of people each year are able to enjoy Dinosaur State Park, and he will always be a hero.

Fossils are the only evidence of dinosaurs that survives—and except for birds, most won't be making any more anytime soon. Treat every fossil with care and they may last another 200 million years.

Keep a few basics in mind while in the field

Remember also a few basic ideas for protecting the environment. What you carry in, carry out. Stay on trails and avoid trampling the ground elsewhere. Take photos and keep a log of your explorations!